PRAISE FOR

SINGING AND DANCING ARE
THE VOICE OF THE LAW

"Busshō Lahn has a flair for metaphor, anecdote, and the one-sentence paragraph. He also has a deft way of holding the Zen tradition, including its formality and ritual, lightly, with real appreciation and understanding born of experience, but without even an ounce of piety. You'll have so much fun reading this book you'll forget how inspiring it is." —**Norman Fischer**, Zen priest and author of *When You Greet Me, I Bow: Notes and Reflections from a Life in Zen*

"This is one of the best books on Zen and Zen practice that I have read in years. Busshō uses a well-known Zen song/poem to elucidate the key features of Zen meditation, practice and life....It brings the famous Zen master's teaching alive while also showing how it is relevant to Zen practice in the 21st century." —**Tim Zentetsu Burkett**, author of *Nothing Holy About It* and *Zen in the Age of Anxiety*

"A deeply personal invitation to dive into your life and awaken your heart of wisdom. With wit and insight, this book calls you into intimacy with yourself and into joyful, authentic, compassionate engagement with what is." —**Ben Connelly**, author of *Inside the Grass Hut* and *Mindfulness and Intimacy*

"In this engaging and insightful book, Busshō Lahn takes us on a deeply personal, and yet universally accessible and resonant journey through Zen practice, and our common spiritual humanity... Anyone interested in the spiritual path, whether they be Zen practitioners or not, will benefit greatly from reading this rich work. Highly recommended." —**Rev. Seifu Singh-Molares**, executive director, Spiritual Directors International

"'Don't miss your life!' It is Busshō Lahn's plea and invitation. This is not a Zen roadmap for your life. Rather, you are being offered a mirror. Look at your life—your suffering, your compassion, your wisdom, your sorrows and joys. Reflect upon your life through Lahn's personal, humble, thoughtful and accessible introduction to the Song of Zazen. In so doing, you just may find delight in the one upon whom you gaze. Yes, and freedom and joy in sharing your life and love with others." —**Rev. Mark S. Hanson**, presiding bishop emeritus, Evangelical Lutheran Church in America

"At some point in reading this book, I stopped taking notes. Then, I stopped reading altogether and simply sat....Singing The Song of Zazen with Busshō Lahn is like surfacing a melody that's been in your bones forever. You find yourself singing with a choirmaster who is wise, funny, surprising—and compassionate beyond measure. Just join the chorus." —**Martha E. Stortz,** professor of religion, Augsburg University

"Lahn invites readers along on a personal and practical journey— venturing from knowing to unknowing, from expert to beginner— towards utilizing the teachings and practices of Zen for not only those who practice it, but also for outsiders seeking deeper insight into the timeless and universal truth, meaning, purpose, connection, and love of the 'beautiful, elegant, humble, and deeply wise tradition' of themselves." —**Hans Gustafson, PhD,** director, Jay Phillips Center for Interreligious Studies, University of St. Thomas

"Busshō Lahn's *Singing and Dancing Are the Voice of the Law* offers an indelible contribution to our understanding of Zen—a wisdom tradition that has enriched my practice of Christianity for over thirty years. This playful and profound teacher doesn't just write about Zen, he shows us Zen-ness. Through his captivating personal stories, Busshō helps us to notice more of the realness and feel more of the rawness in our own experiences. He reminds us that the true test of Zen is

what happens off the cushion. Highly recommended for all those who aspire to live with a beginner's mind and a more compassionate heart."
—**Diane M. Millis, PhD**, author of *Re-Creating a Life* and *Deepening Engagement*

"This book is for me staggering in its depths of wisdom. As I plunged in, I realized not only the power of the words that Hakuin Ekaku's poem carries, but more directly Busshō Lahn's reflections that made them a living text.... I'm deeply indebted to Busshō and this Buddhist wisdom text that brought my own journey closer to myself and my life's experience, and to others as well." —**Rev. Ward Bauman**, director, Episcopal House of Prayer, ret.

SINGING AND DANCING ARE THE VOICE OF THE LAW

A COMMENTARY ON HAKUIN'S "SONG OF ZAZEN"

BUSSHŌ LAHN

INTRODUCTION BY TIM BURKETT

Monkfish Book Publishing Company
Rhinebeck, New York

Paperback ISBN 978-1-948626-78-1
eBook ISBN 978-1-948626-79-8

Library of Congress Cataloging-in-Publication Data

Names: Lahn, Busshō, author. | Burkett, Tim, writer of introduction.
Title: Singing and dancing are the voice of the law : a commentary on
    Hakuin's "Song of Zazen" / Busshō Lahn ; introduction by Tim Burkett.
Description: Rhinebeck : Monkfish Book Publishing Company, 2022.
Identifiers: LCCN 2022019732 (print) | LCCN 2022019733 (ebook) | ISBN
    9781948626781 (paperback) | ISBN 9781948626798 (ebook)
Subjects: LCSH: Hakuin, 1686-1769. Zazen wasan. | Meditation--Zen Buddhism.
    | Buddhist meditations.
Classification: LCC BQ9399.E594 Z393434 2022 (print) | LCC BQ9399.E594
    (ebook) | DDC 294.3/4432--dc23/eng/20220622
LC record available at https://lccn.loc.gov/2022019732
LC ebook record available at https://lccn.loc.gov/2022019733

Book and cover design by Colin Rolfe
Cover painting: "Six Persimmons" (13th century) by Mu Chi

Monkfish Book Publishing Company
22 East Market Street, Suite 304
Rhinebeck, New York 12572
(845) 876-4861
monkfishpublishing.com

CONTENTS

INTRODUCTION

It may seem weird to refer to a book on Zen, or any spiritual teaching, as one that you can't put down. But this was my exact experience after opening this book by Busshō Lahn. Having finished it, I feel deeply grateful for both Hakuin's poetic expression of a joyous stillness, which is at the center of all being, including yours, as well as Busshō's thoughts about how to access it. Busshō shows, time and time again, how, Hakuin, in spite of his reputation as a tough and often cranky Zen master, had a heart-mind both as soft as a baby's and as open as a spring wildflower. As Busshō points this out, he also shows us his own heart-mind.

A feature of this book, which makes it stand out from the hundreds of books that come out every year with a Buddhist-meditation orientation, is Busshō's adeptness at moving between ancient Buddhist teaching and contemporary secular wisdom. He cites a diverse mix of contemporary Americans like David Brooks, writing about Lady Gaga; lyrics by the rock band Duran Duran; and even a psychologist with expertise in dealing with trauma.

A second feature which makes this book stand out is the way it displays the core teachings of Zen with delightful stories from Zen's development in China and Japan, along with Zen's grounding in practices that were brought to China from India more than two thousand years ago, including the Five Remembrances. He clearly elucidates these one by one, showing how their regular recitation has impacted his own spiritual practice and life. He even explains Buddhist terms like *karma*, which often seem complex and confusing, with both clarity and cogency.

As Busshō elaborates on the wisdom displayed in these two features, he punctuates this with a core refrain: We can only discover and open up to the deep wisdom of heart-mind through and from a persistent and patient commitment to Zen meditation (*zazen*).

You may want to read this book from cover to cover in one or two sittings, as I did, or you may prefer to open it and dip into any part of it. It's that good. Hakuin and Busshō have formed a partnership that spans nearly four centuries to show us in myriad ways how to open up to our very own heart-mind, the heart-mind of the universe.

—*Tim Zentetsu Burkett, guiding teacher, Minnesota Zen Center*

PREFACE

By March, 2008, I had heard my Zen teacher, Tim Burkett, give many Dharma talks. Probably dozens at that point, because I'd known him for some years by then. But that particular talk shot through me like an arrow—completely unexpected, searing, transformative, inexplicable. I'm not sure why my heart was so blessedly available that morning, but as he spoke, the hair on the back of my neck raised, an almost-fear response to his volume and passion and message. I became suddenly and acutely aware that I was in public. I wanted to run and I wanted to cry, but I felt I could do neither. The urge to run and the urge to cry are two very common responses to hearing something true, and I had both at once.

Tim was talking about a painting, *Six Persimmons* by Mu Chi, as a Zen Buddhist expression, significant because of its ordinariness. No ethereal realms, no lofty gods or goddesses, no heavens or hells. Just this ordinary fruit, this ordinary moment, this ordinary life. He had a printed copy of the painting with him that he held up as a visual aid. Tim then talked about how quickly something becomes a convention, how quickly we kill something by copying, analyzing, imitating, judging. Then the spontaneity of life is killed.

"When that happens," he said, "tear it up!"

He held his copy of Mu Chi's painting out at arm's length and tore it in half. The sound of paper being ripped apart flew into me like a

flock of restless crows bent on rearranging all my internal furniture. It's hard to say why this particular teaching, a version of which I had heard countless times before, ripped me open so profoundly that day. But right then, that wasn't the point.

The point was that I was in a Zen center, and something felt deeply *right* about what I was experiencing. I was on the right track. I had no idea the size of the project then; in fact, I still don't. But I can tell you that the crazy love crows hidden in that sheet of paper weren't planning anything as tame as rearranging my furniture.

If your spiritual life doesn't have at least a little vein of fear running through it—an awe in the face of the size of *all of this*—then you need to look a little deeper.

The goal of any real spiritual practice is not to rearrange your internal furniture to achieve better traffic flow. It's to tear your house down completely, so that there's nothing between you and love. From the ego's point of view, practice is the least safe thing there is. Good. That's the point. Love isn't about safe. Love is about love.

THE FIRE OF TRUTH

I blame my sister for all this.

My sister is either directly or indirectly responsible for introducing me to the three most crucially good things in my life: Zen, my teacher, and my wife, in that order. And as crucially good as those three things are, they are also the most inconvenient, life-altering, world-shaking things I've had relationships with. The really good stuff is always a massive inconvenience, I've learned, and if something or someone isn't bent on turning your life inside out, it's probably not that valuable.

So my sister won't be surprised to hear me blaming her for all the inconvenience I've experienced as a result of her interferences because, as an older brother, I've been unfairly blaming her for all kinds of my various difficulties her whole life. It's what siblings tend to do, and at this point, it's like a tradition.

When I was twenty-three, my sister lent me a book she wanted me to read: *The Three Pillars of Zen* by Philip Kapleau. It had been the course text for a class she'd taken in college called "Zen Meditation and the Question of Time." That's a pretty provocative title for a college class, and the book was no less so.

I refused the book when she first offered it because (and I remember saying this), "It sounds like religion." I still think that response is funny, given what my life looks like now, but at the time I was most certainly not looking for a new religion, or any religion for that matter.

But I didn't understand religion any more than I understood anything else, so I wasn't a good judge of what I needed and what I didn't.

Anyway, I ended up reading her stupid book. And it lit my head on fire. It was completely fascinating and pulled at me in a very unusual way. The book is full of descriptions of strict, grueling monastic practice, huge amounts of formal, seated meditation (zazen), and—best of all—dramatic enlightenment experiences. I had no idea religion could show up that way.

Wow, I thought, *that's for me.*

I wanted more, so I went to the library and grabbed the first book I found in the tiny section on Zen Buddhism: *Zen Mind, Beginner's Mind* by Shunryu Suzuki. It couldn't have been more different than the Kapleau book, but I loved it even more. To this day, when I'm asked the "If you could have only one book on a desert island" question, that's the one. It's kaleidoscopic to me, with endless corridors and changing landscapes in it. And it did for my heart what the Kapleau book did for my head: it lit it on fire.

I remember laughing aloud while reading it that first time, knowing it wasn't objectively funny, knowing that Suzuki Roshi (*roshi* is a term of respect for a great Zen teacher) had contradicted himself three times in the same short paragraph—something about form being emptiness, but also being form, and neither, or something like that. It made no sense.

But my feeling was that Suzuki Roshi wasn't trying to be deep, inscrutable, or (heaven forbid) "Zen." He was just doing his utmost to persuade language to convey a truth that it couldn't.

My laugh was from someplace I couldn't understand, and my body felt hot and awake and afraid and joyful. And I spoke aloud to no one, perhaps to everyone, maybe just to myself, "This is the first true thing I've ever read."

I didn't know it, but I feared it: my life had changed, and I was on a new trajectory.

We tend to be terrified of meeting something deep and true because then we are compelled to change our lives to match it as best we can.

Encountering truth, whether in words, art, music, in nature or in a person, is extraordinarily inconvenient. Inconvenient, that is, unless we ignore it, which we most often do, which is what I did, at least for a time.

Zen had my scent in its nose by then, though, and it began a long, patient stalking. I never had a chance.

THE SONG OF ZAZEN

I don't remember when I first came across Hakuin's poem, Song of Zazen. I started my study and practice of Zen Buddhism in 1993, and I likely would have read about Hakuin ("HAH-koo-in") in my first few years of study. Hakuin saw deep compassion and commitment to help all living beings as an indispensable part of the Buddhist path to awakening. He was a hugely influential figure in Japanese Zen in the 1700s, the archetypal Zen master of the people, who extended his teaching far beyond the monastery to include people from all walks of life. In his day, Hakuin was to Japanese Zen what the Beatles were to rock'n'roll in the 1960s. He was a radical reformer, reinvigorating the active practice of Zen, both within the monasteries and among the common folk. He was hugely popular, traveling and lecturing across Japan, and his temple drew masses. Whereas most teachers of his day would have had one or two successors, Hakuin trained over eighty. (On the other hand, he never toured North America and his face didn't end up on thousands of t-shirts, so the Beatles analogy only goes so far.)

Despite the loftiness of Hakuin's status, the villagers he visited on lecture tours saw him as their spiritual grandfather. And in the Song of Zazen, I find a beautiful poem that celebrates the sanctity of the everyday. His words give me the feeling of simple transcendence that we encounter when we manage to mentally catch a glimpse of ourselves in the middle of a warm, loving moment of gratitude.

The Song of Zazen isn't a stadium anthem to be chanted by thousands; it's more like John Lennon's "Julia," a tender, personal contemplation that isn't as well-known but that immediately expands the hearts of those lucky enough to hear it.

In fact, its spirit goes past Zen. Many of these same teachings can be found throughout the world, both inside and out of the world's faith traditions.

So, although I'm a Zen teacher and I come from a Zen point of view, I see Hakuin's Song of Zazen as a heartfelt offering to a suffering world, not just to suffering Buddhists. Suffering isn't Buddhist, it's human. It's universal. No exceptions. And the Bodhisattva vows to relieve suffering—the vows that fueled Hakuin's life and that we still chant every day in Zen—apply to all beings. All beings. No exceptions.

Some years back, I came across a copy of Hakuin's Song of Zazen again in an old collection of papers at Zen Center, and the first stanza was immediately arresting, as challenging as it was comforting. It felt like Tim's *Six Persimmons* Dharma talk all over again, tearing into my chest. I decided there was important teaching in it for me, so I made a copy of that old page and added it to my morning chant list. I wanted to know more about Hakuin, the famous and intimidating Zen master, and what his words might sound like coming out of my mouth, in my voice.

What follows in this book is a bit of what the Song of Zazen has moved in me. I'll use it as a jumping-off place to explore the things it's helped me see, feel, know, and un-know.

It takes away far more than it gives, thank goodness, because the last thing most of us need is *more*. It seems to me that what most of us need, desperately, is *less*. A *lot* less.

WHAT IS A TEACHER?

It's good for you to know that my intention is not to offer anything authoritative on either Hakuin's Song of Zazen or the tradition from which it springs, Zen Buddhism. I do not pretend to be a scholar or an expert on the Japanese cultural expression of Zen Buddhism, especially not Hakuin's tradition.

I've practiced Zen long enough to know that there is no such thing as an authority on Zen. Claiming to be one would be akin to being an authority on life, on breathing, on the spaces behind black holes, on the ankles of ants. Nope.

Scholarship, even rigorous and authoritative scholarship, has a place in religion, and Zen is no exception. But Zen knows that if we're not careful, we can have a tendency to let careful observation become dissecting scrutiny, and the things we're observing can lose their life. In our desire to know, we can have a tendency to pin butterflies to boards and attach made-up Latin names to them, rather than appreciate and wonder about the colorful miracle insect flying in crazy loops past us.

So Zen is the opposite. We see what we've pinned to boards and we take the pins out. We go from understanding a butterfly's flight patterns and migratory routes to just watching in wonder as something colorful flits around flowers.

We go from *I know* to *I don't know*. We go from Latin names to no names. We go from being an expert to being a beginner, and then eventually to forgetting that there's a difference.

And please don't misunderstand—Zen is not an anti-intellectual practice. In fact, it's famously rigorous, both physically and academically. But Zen understands that there are many ways of knowing. And knowing with the brain is only one. And it's an important one, but it's also limited. In Zen, we practice wisdom, compassion, and service. In other words, we see, we feel, and we try to help. In that order.

I say that I'm a teacher, but I don't know what that is. No one does. We talk about it like we know, but we don't. We've all had teachers, both ones we'd call good and ones we'd call bad. Perhaps we have a metric that makes sense to us in deciding which were which: what our grades and test scores were while working with that teacher, how much fun we had in that setting, how much we liked what they were trying to teach us, how they made us feel.

But there are no tests in Zen, nor grades as such. The setting is our lives, and what Zen teachers are trying to teach us is vague at best: "A feeling for life," or something like that.

So, beyond the obvious extremes, it's pretty hard to tell not only who's good and who's not good at teaching Zen, but it's also hard to tell who the teachers actually are and what it is that's actually being taught.

Teachers can only offer what they are. They can help us to learn and help us to unlearn what's in our way. But at some point in practice, we need to really understand that our real teacher is our life—every part of it.

NO FIXED STARS

When I'm talking about Zen, I tend to use sweeping generalizations, which is sometimes helpful and sometimes not. Generalizations help us see patterns in the big picture, and that's why I love them. I know there's an exception to every rule and that every particle has its uniqueness, but I like seeing the flow, the patterns that underlie the details, the trends that inform the specifics. And when it comes to Zen practice, I think that's all we can actually do. Sure, every teacher and temple has their own melody, but I'm more interested in the overall harmony of the piece, how it all connects and comes together.

Absolute truth can't actually be spoken or written, so words don't work anyway.

For years (no kidding: years), I wanted Truth to be reducible to something unchanging, a simple (and hopefully pithy) saying that would always be true, always. Like most humans, I want a fixed star, something to rely on, something that never moves and is always true.

If I look very carefully at why I want that so badly, at what is underneath all those desires for clarity and certainty, I eventually find fear. Of course. I seek clarity because I'm unclear, and that's scary. I seek certainty because I'm uncertain and that's scary. I want a fixed star because I feel lost on a very, very big ocean.

And in Zen, insights are really just medicine, applied to specific conditions at specific times. No medicine works for all diseases, and yesterday's Dharma is exactly that: yesterday's Dharma. It might be applicable today; it might not. In my experience, most of yesterday's

Dharma is still just as relevant today as it was hundreds of years ago. But some of it isn't.

In seeking a "cure" for my fear, my underlying assumption must be some variation on the theme that feeling fear means something is wrong and needs to be fixed.

But is that true? Sometimes. Sometimes not. In fact, often not.

Even if I did somehow find an actual fixed star, would my fear be erased? No, just assuaged, because my fearlessness is still dependent on that star. If it went away or I stopped being able to see it, my fear would return. My fear isn't understood and transformed, it's just asleep.

This doesn't mean we make up whatever suits us today because we're in the mood and call it "Dharma." Zen isn't a spineless or traditionless tradition. Quite the opposite. Like most religious traditions, it takes its traditional elements very seriously, and with good reason. But at the core of Zen is also the embracing of Great Doubt, the living moment, the recognition that our response to the eternally unfolding Reality can't be static but must be spontaneous, genuine, wholehearted. The true Dharma can't stay seated for long, because both the content and context of Moment are eternally dynamic. Even fixed stars aren't fixed. In real life, they're not only moving at thousands of miles an hour through space—the light we see, which we call a "star," was burned into existence thousands of years ago and is passing us at 186,000 miles per second.

No fixed stars.

At least, none outside of us.

More on that later.

CAST OF CHARACTERS

Many years after that first reading of Suzuki Roshi's book, I found my Zen teacher. His name is Tim Zentetsu Burkett, and he was one of Suzuki Roshi's early students. After practicing for a few years, Suzuki Roshi instructed Tim to start a sitting group in his hometown of Palo

Alto, California. It was at that small sitting group that Suzuki Roshi delivered the talks that would become *Zen Mind, Beginner's Mind*.

Tim told me, "We only sit for the benefit of all beings," which is a sentence that would fit effortlessly into his teacher's book and sums up nicely the vows and the spirit of our Zen practice.

In this book, you'll notice some Zen-sounding names that pop up as I draw on wisdom I've learned from my teachers and others who've gone before me and alongside me. Here are some of the names you'll see most often:

- Hakuin Ekaku, of course, is the author of the Song of Zazen, which we'll be exploring together. Easily one of the most well-known of all Zen masters, Hakuin's famously rigorous practice belied a huge and tender heart, which is the part of him that I feel wrote Song of Zazen, and the part of him I trust the most.

- Shunryu Suzuki, as you'll recall, is the author of *Zen Mind, Beginner's Mind*, and was my teacher's first teacher. Many books have been written by or about him, and deservedly so. The early paperback editions of *Zen Mind, Beginner's Mind* had an informally taken picture of his face on the entirety of the back cover, and I spent as much time studying that picture as I did reading the text. To me, both the firm clarity of his wisdom and the kind compassion of his heart were in full view. When I quote him in the coming pages, I'm probably drawing from *Zen Mind, Beginner's Mind* or *Not Always So*. I call him Suzuki Roshi as a term of respect and gratitude for his influence in my life.

- Dainin Katagiri, my teacher's second teacher, founded the Minnesota Zen Meditation Center (MZMC), where I spent my formational practice years and received my formal training. Katagiri Roshi came to the US in the '60s as a Japanese Zen missionary, working in Los Angeles and San Francisco before bringing his teaching to the Midwest, and was the first Zen master to take up residence between California and New York. He had already died by the time I first visited MZMC in 1993, but my practicing in that very same building where he had lived with his wife and sons, practiced zazen morning and night, taught Zen, walked, ate, laughed, wept, and breathed for fourteen years connected me to him and his lineage in a way I find difficult to express.

- Eihei Dogen was a Japanese Zen monk in the 1200s whose writings are still a clear and powerful expression of Zen practice. Dogen is one of the most extraordinary, most poetic, most profound voices and exemplars in Zen. These days, with much of his work finally translated into English and widely available, it's a happy fact that his religious poetry, essays, and talks are being discovered and studied by students and practitioners of many faiths, and the depth of his insight and expression is finally being recognized beyond the circles of Japanese Zen.

ANCIENT TEACHINGS IN A MODERN WORLD

I sometimes wonder why an American like myself, born and raised Catholic, would even try to understand moments of religious insight through the practice and lens of Zen Buddhism, or conversely, why I would attempt to understand Zen through my everyday, twenty-first-century life.

In his beautiful book *Honey from the Rock*, Rabbi Lawrence Kushner talks about his own tradition of Kabbalah and how contemporary Kabbalists are integrating an ancient and profoundly culture-bound religion with a contemporary, essentially nonreligious culture. He writes, "One can be, if not a Kabbalist, then at least their legitimate and reverent heir, even in this day. The ancient mysteries still instruct us."

The ancient traditions of insight, contemplation, wisdom, and compassion are as alive now as they have ever been. The kind of wisdom that is expressed by the awakened heart-mind exists outside of time and is not limited by the tradition or culture that may attempt to hold it.

The search for truth, meaning, purpose, connection, love—these are universal and timeless. The way we search and the symbols we use change, but the impulse is eternal.

INFINITY IS YOURS

When we go far outside on a clear night, away from light pollution, we can stare up into the depths of the night sky. We are gazing at infinity. Even if we gaze at that infinity through a cardboard toilet-paper tube, although our field of vision significantly smaller, we still see infinity. It's no less infinite than the unobstructed view, because even a tiny fraction of infinity is still infinite.

Your toilet-paper-tube view is limited. Your toilet-paper-tube view also still beholds the ultimate sky. There is only one sky, and your limited view sees it. The one moon shows in every pool, and in every pool, the one moon. There is therefore only one seeing. It is yours and it is not "yours," because it is not limited to you.

So the view you have from your cushion is not yours. It is the only view, it is all views, so it belongs to all beings.

Considering the scope and depth of what I'm trying to write about with this book, the best I can hope for is a toilet-paper-tube vision. But that's okay. I'll do my best. And a fraction is only a fraction, but it's also the whole.

Speaking of behalf of others is always dangerous, and I try not to do it. I even hesitate to speak on behalf of myself, but I'll do just that with this offering, in the hopes that something here can catalyze a helpful connection being made in your heart about suffering, Zen, or life. That is my hope.

I hope this book helps to entice you to explore and practice this beautiful, elegant, humble, and deeply wise tradition for yourself. Or don't. Either decision is fine, either is complete.

And my hope is that you feel some of the fire that was in Hakuin's heart as your own. Trace the tongue of invisible flame down through the ages. Claim it as your own, because it is. It can't belong to anyone else.

THE SONG OF ZAZEN

HAKUIN EKAKU (1686-1769)

TRANSLATED BY NORMAN WADDELL,
USED BY PERMISSION

All beings by nature are Buddha,
As ice by nature is water.
Apart from water there is no ice;
Apart from beings, no Buddha.

How sad that people ignore the near
And search for truth afar:
Like someone in the midst of water
Crying out in thirst,
Like a child of a wealthy home
Wandering among the poor.

Lost on dark paths of ignorance,
We wander through the Six Worlds,
From dark path to dark path—
When shall we be freed from birth and death?

Oh, the zazen of the Mahayana!
To this the highest praise!
Devotion, repentance, training,
The many paramitas—
All have their source in zazen.

Those who try zazen even once
Wipe away beginningless crimes.
Where are all the dark paths then?
The Pure Land itself is near.

Those who hear this truth even once
And listen with a grateful heart,
Treasuring it, revering it,
Gain blessings without end.

Much more, those who turn about
And bear witness to self-nature,
Self-nature that is no-nature,
Go far beyond mere doctrine.

Here effect and cause are the same,
The Way is neither two nor three.

With form that is no-form,
Going and coming, we are never astray.

With thought that is no-thought,
Singing and dancing are the voice of the Law.

Boundless and free is the sky of Samádhi!
Bright the full moon of wisdom!

Truly, is anything missing now?
Nirvana is right here, before our eyes,
This very place is the Lotus Land,
This very body, the Buddha.

1

S I N G

THE MAGIC OF SONG

Let's start at the beginning, with the Song's title: Song of Zazen.

This ancient piece of Zen poetry touches me in a different way because it's called a song. If this piece was called a *teaching*, a *poem*, or even *wisdom*, we might brace ourselves against it somehow, or prepare ourselves for it with our expectations of what many teachings, poems, and offerings of wisdom are: mostly boring.

But we start with the word *song*. A nice word, a word I think most of us like. Even saying the word *song* can make us feel good. It can lower our defenses. Music enters and moves us when we allow it to. Actually, it enters and moves us when we don't, too. It's subtle and pervasive and magic.

Songs don't wish to correct us or control us or teach us. They want to seduce us! They draw at us from a faraway place that's within us already, and they coax us onward toward more awareness, toward deeper feeling, toward integration, toward wholeness.

The "deeper feeling" part is important. Music is designed to help us feel more deeply, more completely, more powerfully. To remind us of the size and scope of the emotional undercurrent of our lives. In short, the vast majority of music is designed to be a lens through which to experience life: sadness, joy, trance, bliss, anger, exploration, curiosity, tenderness. A song is a tapestry of emotion that we become part of for a few minutes. We try it on like a new outfit. And like an outfit, it can help us notice parts of ourselves we wouldn't have known existed otherwise.

Our human hearts seem almost always open to a song. We need lullabies, rock'n'roll, singer-songwriter stuff, Mozart, ancient folk songs, birdsong, and Doomtree. We need our own (perhaps secret) tenacious habit of playing the tin whistle or ukulele to ourselves when no one else is home, or our loud and heartfelt version of "R-E-S-P-E-C-T" in the shower.

THE MAGIC OF SONG

Zazen is the next word in our Song, and we need to understand what zazen is and what it isn't.

Zazen (simply meaning *seated Zen*) is traditional Zen Buddhist meditation. It's the primary type of meditation that you'll find at a Zen center, and it is always practiced in silence, with no guidance offered. (I include some basic instructions for zazen in the appendix for reference.)

Unlike most forms of meditation, zazen has no agenda for us and doesn't need to look or feel a certain way. Zazen is a form of meditation in which the practitioner does not use any specific object of meditation; rather, practitioners remain as much as possible in the present moment, aware of and observing what moves in and around them. It's simple but profound, taking only a few minutes to learn but a lifetime to master.

The word *meditation* is a lot like the word *exercise*. It can mean a lot of things, and they're all a little bit different. There are many types of specific activities and practices that could be included in the broad category of "meditation," and there are perhaps an equal number of particular objectives for all those different things.

But for right now, it might be helpful for us to think of the types of meditation as falling into two main categories: *calming* and *understanding.* (The Sanskrit origin terms for these categories are *samatha* and *vipassana*, which are usually translated as "calming/centering," and "insight into.")

The first category, *calming*, is pretty straightforward. Generally speaking, when most folks hear the word meditation, it's some form of samatha that's being talking about. These are the kinds of meditation practices that are intended to result in feeling less stress, strain, and difficulty. They can lower blood pressure and heart rate, calm our jangled nervous system, and bring about pain relief. Even though there's effort involved, they are generally more passive practices, and they can help us to calm our busy brains and feel grounded and safe.

The second category, *understanding*, is less common, but still pretty straightforward to describe. These vipassana insight practices are literally that: insight into and understanding of our own heart-mind and reality itself. We might say that they're devoted to clear seeing, deep comprehension, and revealing the truth by being in relationship with what actually is. They're more active. We not only experience what is arising in the field of our awareness, but we can also *know* it. We can see its true nature, its origins, and how it connects to other things.

Perhaps you can already intuit how too much of one, without a balance of the other, is limited in its ability to help us grow in our awareness. Just samatha on its own can easily become simple escapism, a spiritual hot tub, magical thinking, a form of fantasy. It feels great while you're in it, but as soon as the bell rings, reality reasserts itself and nothing has changed. It's just heaven, but no earth. Mindfulness without understanding and integration is simply self-soothing, a reaction to a symptom, a painkiller.

When we're saturated with pain, the calming, symptom-management variety of meditation is merciful and appropriate, like giving codeine to someone after a root canal.

But codeine after a tough workday? Because of a traffic jam? Very few people actually need calming, soothing meditation because of a parking ticket or a difficult phone call. We need to instead use our mindfulness to investigate what we're experiencing. Suffering has causes, and unless and until we compassionately and wisely relate to both the suffering and its cause, it will simply come back again later, and nothing will change.

On the other hand, too much insight practice on its own, without the balance of relaxation's softness, can become rigid, analytical, judgmental, and even harsh. Suddenly, we're not in meditation anymore, we're lost in thoughts, analysis, system theories, and criticism. Our minds become constricted and we lose our possibility for growth and expansion. Our ego identity, based on its old story and fears, can assert itself and we'll start to take ourselves too seriously. We spin around and around in our heads, or around and around in our pain. We lose our perspective and our spaciousness.

These two kinds of meditation can be done separately or together, and some types of meditation—like zazen—can fall into both categories simultaneously. And ultimately we want to practice both at once, to be calm and centered yet comprehending and insightful. We wish to be relaxed enough in our awareness to be open, accepting, allowing, unattached, and nonjudgmental. We also wish to be attentive enough to be alert, engaged, aware, curious, and clear in our understanding.

Thus, in the shortest version of zazen instruction I've ever heard, my teacher simply says, "Relax and pay attention."

She's told me that hundreds of times.

INFINITE, ORDINARY, AND IRREPLACEABLE

Zazen is not part of a self-improvement project, nor is it a means to an end. Our relationship with zazen is not like our relationship with an exercise routine, responsible spending, or healthy eating. True spiritual practice is dedication to the activities of our everyday life. A devotion to the ordinary; a vow to see it as extraordinary.

Our zazen is far more art than craft, far more expression than technique, far more universal than personal. Zazen, like music, is an offering for a world with an unquenchable thirst for its expression of awareness, compassion, uprightness, balance, dignity, poise, compassion, receptivity, and equanimous kindness. In short, zazen is the most profound expression of religious devotion in the Zen Buddhist tradition. "Zazen is not limited to the practice of sitting alone," Dogen reminds us; it doesn't begin with one bell and end with another, it's your life. It's an infinite expression of the heart-mind.

I'll try to remember to say this again at the end of the book because I think it's so important: The Song of Zazen isn't a dusty old poem written by a boring, long-dead Zen teacher. The Song of Zazen is your song. You bring Zen alive—not Hakuin or Thich Nhat Hanh or Buddha or anyone else you think is spiritually special. It's you, your posture, your heart-mind united that brings Zen alive and brings you alive.

There is no Zen without zazen, without practice. Reading about Zen is like reading about swimming. It can be helpful insofar as it gets you to the pool. But without the pool and swimmer, there is no swimming. So if you only have a half-hour today for your practice, put this book down and go do zazen. Face the wall, face yourself. Become what arises when you vanish.

That's Zen, and it cannot be found in this book or any other.

There is no replacement in all creation for your zazen. Only you can do it, only you can offer it, only you can sing it, and only you can become it.

YOU ARE BUDDHA

All beings by nature are Buddha,
As ice by nature is water.
Apart from water there is no ice;
Apart from beings, no Buddha.

Our song starts with a sledgehammer blow to our usual understandings of meditation, Buddha, and ourselves. *All beings by nature are Buddha.* A powerful and brave first line. Even now, thousands of years after it was first given, and 250 years after Hakuin expressed it as he did in his Song, it is still a startling teaching.

But before we can really understand it, we need to talk about ice cubes.

OUR ESSENTIAL NATURE IS ONENESS

Apart from water there is no ice. When ice cubes are in a tray, we can imagine that they're separate. If we pour them into a bowl and let them melt, we can see another part of that, another part of reality. "Not one, not two," we say in Zen.

No, we're not all "one." When I scratch my arm, you can't feel it. If we weren't separate beings, we wouldn't have to ask each other where it hurts. But that separateness is only half the truth, like the heads side of a coin. And without the tails side—non-separateness—we don't get all the truth, either.

We're being told about two perspectives on existence, two dimensions of reality, the Relative and the Absolute. They are like our two eyes. They are both 100 percent correct, and they both see only part of the truth. But we need both to see fully, to see with depth and distance. Each of the two perspectives helps, supports, and enlightens the other.

The relative dimension reminds us of our own uniqueness, our own personal experience of Reality. We experience ourselves as separate beings, moving around, bumping into things, trying to grab some things and push others away. The human experience. This is light as *the particle*.

The relative is the place we live most of the time, so it comes pretty easy for us. That's part of why the Song starts by reminding us of the absolute—we need a lot more education and reminding about that one.

The absolute dimension reminds of our ultimate interconnectedness. The essential water nature of ice, the inherent undividedness-from-water that we know it already contains.

We know what happens to ice cubes in a water glass after a while. They stop being separate. And it was always their nature to do so. All that was needed was a temperature change for them to remember their unity. This is light as *the wave*.

In Zen, zazen is the heat that melts our ice cube ideas into water ideas, melts our little separate selves into Buddha. And we go back and forth, back and forth, because we're already both, ice and water, particle and wave.

And in Zen—and this is a biggie, so pay attention—*one isn't seen as better, higher, or more advanced than the other.* In fact, we feel and know in our own cells how water often shows up: as ice!

We can make peace with our essential ice nature, just like we can make peace with our essential water nature. We can make peace with our human nature, knowing that it's also—fully and completely—Buddha Nature. We feel and know in our own cells how Buddha usually shows up: as us!

All beings by nature are Buddha. Our usual difficulty with this teaching is the word *all.*

Perhaps it's easy to think that Buddha was inherently Buddha. Or Jesus or Mohammed or Mother Teresa or the Dalai Lama, Saint Teresa or Desmond Tutu.

But what about you? You, and your crazy ping-pong brain, and your dumpster-fire life? Are you able to imagine that you're included in the category Buddha by Nature? What about Donald Trump? Oprah? Isaac Newton? Harriet Tubman? Lao Tsu? Joan of Arc? Eleanor Roosevelt? Gandhi? Queen Elizabeth? Your neighbor? Your mother? The person who sold you this book?

Imagine that you are included. Imagine that enlightenment and full Buddhahood are your inheritance and that there is no table in the universe at which you do not already have a reserved seat.

All beings are Buddha. You are a being. Therefore, you are Buddha. By nature, by birthright, inherently, fully.

And then let those ideas go and practice. Come back to your own body, your own breath, your own suffering, your own beating heart. Believing "I am Buddha" is not the point and is of little help. The whole of creation realizing itself and verifying itself through you is the point. So use your imagination to help fuel your practice, but don't stop at beliefs or ideas. Sit zazen and realize its truth.

WHAT IS A BEING?

All beings by nature are Buddha. It's interesting that Hakuin hasn't said "people" yet. We humans don't arrive until the next stanza. He's just said *all beings.*

What is a being?

Are rocks beings? Are viruses? Are clouds? Are emotions? Are thoughts? Are ideas?

Is the past a being? How about the future?

These are good questions, and well worth asking—up to a point. But don't get stuck in that dissection. Dissecting that much can kill. I'm not saying not to look closely—do some musing about those questions. But don't get lost, don't stay in your head—and *please* don't land on any firm answers.

To be clear, I'm not saying that that kind of knowing is bad. I'm saying that your left frontal cortex is a knife and you need to be careful how you use it. A dagger in the hands of an angry man and a scalpel in the hands of a surgeon are both knives, but they are very different things.

Those speculative questions can be used to expand consciousness with our imagination, which is helpful up to a point. But if that's all we do, we're lost in the abstract and we're ignoring the very real feelings that give rise to those questions in the first place, and no healing can happen.

But speculative questions can also be—and very often are—an attempt to limit the unlimited and to divide what is not divided.

We humans really want to know who's in the club and who's out, don't we? Why? What is that?

Well, we're tribal animals, so belonging is a big deal for us. Knowing we're included—that we're accepted in the tribe—is akin to survival itself. Being "in" means being safe. It means surviving. So a good portion of our desire to draw those lines is simple fear. We fear what we do not know, and so we want to know. And that's fine. But when we ignore or are unaware of the motivator for our questioning—fear—we stop seeing how that fear informs what we're likely to discover with our inquiry.

This just shows you your mind. If you imagine that you've found a being, then it's included in Buddha. If you imagine that you've found something that isn't a being, then you've found a being, and it's included in Buddha.

All beings includes the Great Earth. *All beings* means all beings.

All beings are Buddha means that existence itself has, no *is*, awakening nature.

HEADS *AND* TAILS

Buddha is a target you cannot miss, a target you already are. No target!

Buddha is a project we cannot fail at; it's already fully completed. No project!

And yet it's a very real project, and one that can't be skipped over by the assertion, "I'm already Buddha." As Shunryu Suzuki Roshi said, "You're already perfect just as you are. And you could use a little improvement."

The second part of this—the needing improvement part—is easy for us. We understand that we suffer, that on some level we're a mess, that our lives often feel barely held together. So it's the first part—the already perfect part—that we don't get. We don't get it because we don't feel it.

And even harder for us to hold is the entire statement, both parts, at once and feel them both as true. The only thing to do is take a breath, center ourselves in what we call *beginner's mind*, and work with it until we can feel the whole thing as true and practice our lives from that place of understanding.

Trying to live with only one perspective on reality is like trying to hand someone just the heads side of a coin. "The man holding a hammer sees a world filled with only nails," as the old saying goes, and we're good at hitting nails hard and long before realizing that they're screws. If you're trying to conceive a child, all you see are babies. If you're lonely, you only see couples. If you sell shoes, you just see people's shoes. So it's important to notice when we're sticking to a single perspective. But we insist on doing just that, taking just one perspective, pretty much all the time. Think about how subtle and pervasive this is:

"That guy is a bully."

"My mother is a saint."

"War is hell."

"What a beautiful sunrise!"

Whenever we claim that something or someone *is* one thing and not another, we're choosing to ignore a bunch of other perspectives. "That guy is a bully" certainly implies that he's not not-a-bully, and "war is hell" implies that no good can come from it. But there isn't a bully in world who isn't sometimes nice. There isn't a saintly mother in the world who isn't sometimes unsaintly. And war, as filled with terror as it is, is also filled with other things, too: love, courage, resiliency, hope.

Non-separateness includes constant dynamic change and no abiding anything. That's why the bully isn't a bully. It's more accurate to say, "He's being a bully" or "He's acting like a bully right now."

When we insist upon abiding qualities, we are simplifying the world to meet our own need for a graspable reality and world that makes sense. We love to do this. In fact, thinking itself is inherently this very thing: simplification, picking and choosing, creating a story to believe in. Thoughts, like words, are symbols that represent what we imagine to be reality. But they are not reality. They are often close enough to be of enormous help to us, which is why we keep doing it. But thoughts and ideas, including the idea of permanence and separateness, are only a useful fiction. Comedian Maria Bamford calls this fiction "a construct to help compartmentalize chaos." Same thing.

All experience is non-abiding. *Thus, a state of consciousness is non-abiding.* Not even the Buddha's enlightenment is abiding. (As Suzuki Roshi says, "Strictly speaking, there are no enlightened beings. There is only enlightened activity.")

TRANSCENDENT EXPERIENCE IS ONLY AN EXPERIENCE

As intense and potentially catalytic as a big spiritual experience can be, it doesn't necessarily transform us. For most folks, having a great high is just that: a great high. And when we come down, we come right back to the place and person we were before we had the high. We might have had a great time, but we're not changed by it. It's like going skydiving to have a big experience. Suzuki Roshi called this "dry enlightenment," because generally speaking, after the high wears off, we're back where we started. In fact, for many folks, trying to get the high back becomes such a distraction that their practice is compromised for a while after a big experience.

There have been many tremendously gifted spiritual teachers who had regular access to lofty and "transcendent" states of consciousness but who also collected Rolls Royces despite teaching simplicity, and who slept with their students despite teaching against misusing sexuality. How could this be, we wonder?

If we're healthy, we grow as we age: physically, emotionally, mentally, and spiritually. Our *stage of development* is the place we live most of the time and it changes throughout our life as we grow on the path of self-individuation and realization. It's like being in school and knowing that you're at a very different place in ninth grade than you were in third grade. You're more developed, more advanced, more independent, and more capable. And under good conditions, this upward growth arc is pretty steady for most folks, although there are many variables and a large spectrum of experience.

Our stage of development is closely tied to our ego identity and our sense of self. So on the spiritual/religious path, we'd expect to be in a more advanced place ten years from now than we are now. If we keep up our practice, we'd expect to be in a different *stage of development*.

But *state of consciousness* adds in another variable. All of us, every day, regardless of age or stage of development, move through many states of consciousness, back and forth between being childish and wise, between being selfish and magnanimous, between being loving and hateful. Grown adults with mature and stable personalities can fly into a rage given the right circumstantial trigger. Suddenly they're a tantrum-throwing two-year old trying to get their most basic needs met. They're in a different state of consciousness than they usually are, and they perceive the world and act on it in a very different way.

It's the same even with higher states of consciousness. We can be a pretty normal person and, given the right circumstances, have an intense experience of awakening (or enlightenment, *kensho, satori,* Big

Mind, breakthrough, rapture, bliss, Presence, etc.). We might even see and experience that we are all water, underneath our perceptions of being ice.

But it's sadly common to see teachers, gurus, priests, or people with spiritual role power—people who generally do have some access to lofty states of consciousness and truth—also have deep splits in them that come out sideways as misuse of power, sexuality, financial extortion, or simple greed. The deep suffering they carry that gives rise to those hurtful behaviors has remained unaddressed—or insufficiently addressed—by their spiritual practice and they can remain, at least to some degree, disengaged with the whole truth of who they are. When the exalted state of consciousness passes, they return to where their center of gravity really is: being a hurt kid with lots of unmet needs. By using spiritual practice, they've bypassed the real pain, the real work.

Simply put, their states of consciousness don't match their stage of development. So they inevitably return from their meditative trance and go back to being caught by their own suffering, their old unmet needs, and their unexamined and painful personal karma. They haven't done what a Western psychologist might call their "shadow work," and so their integration is incomplete. They are essentially split beings, caught between the lofty spiritual state of consciousness and the gravity of their unhealed wounds, their actual stage of personal development.

Some schools of meditation prize experiences of higher consciousness, and some forms of meditation are designed specifically to attempt to bring them about. But in Soto Zen the emphasis is placed on doing the daily work of practice, as that's what moves us along in our stage of development. We spend less time on states of consciousness, calling them the "scenery" of both meditation and life. And that's not to diminish their importance, but rather to change our relationship with them.

Our tendency to slide into a specific state of consciousness can tell us a lot about our inner world and where our energy needs to go. It can tell us about where our suffering is, where our limits are. In any given day, we go from being ice to water and back again many times. All of us. The practice is to see it, to know it, and to investigate those movements with great interest, great kindness, and great care. That's the activity of the by-nature Buddha that Hakuin promises that we already are.

Hakuin's brilliant metaphor for this awakened consciousness, "As ice by nature is water," invites us into a different relationship with our suffering. We're assured that our suffering—the places in us that are frozen, constricted, stuck, trapped—can return to the state of water, dynamic and free-flowing.

And how does ice become water? We all know the answer to that.

So, let's take Hakuin seriously, and let's do a simple exercise to explore, in our immediate felt experience, the central metaphor of his poem.

In your imagination (or with your body), hold a little ice cube.
1. *How do you feel after holding the ice cube for a few minutes?*
2. *What's the instinct of your body?*
3. *What happens if you just keep holding the ice cube, patiently and tenderly?*
4. *What melts the ice?*
5. *Where does that heat come from?*

The answers are obvious and universal:
1. *We feel pain.*
2. *Our body's instinct is to drop the ice cube, to throw it away.*
3. *If we don't, it begins to melt and turn back into water.*
4. *Our natural, effortless body heat is what melts that ice.*
5. *And that heat comes from our blood, warmed and circulated by our heart.*

What a simple and lovely analogy. If we obey our lower instincts, we drop our suffering.

That's what the body will always do: avoid what hurts. But our higher functions of self—like the presence of simple kindness and compassion—have the opposite instinct: they move towards suffering, immediately, without delay, doubt, or reservation. Our highest self—our Buddha self—can befriend and tame our lower functions when necessary, in service of awareness and love.

The body says, avoid what hurts. But compassion says, I'll be with you, even when you hurt.

And compassion isn't a new, foreign quality we need to discover or find or create. Sure, we can clarify and strengthen it, but it's there already, as the natural heat of our body is already there, already complete. We don't need to create it. We already are it.

BREATHE IN SAMENESS, BREATHE OUT DIFFERENCE

As I've said, in Zen, daily practice is the essential thing. Chanting is a regular and important part of my daily practice, as it has been for spiritual practitioners for thousands of years, so let me put in a whole-hearted recommendation for chanting practice here. (I've added more on the specifics of chanting practice in the Appendix.) It's a beautiful way to embody the sameness and difference of ice and water, Absolute and Relative, non-separateness and separateness.

When we chant, we unify sameness and difference. We breathe in what we call *air*, emptiness, the non-specific, general, the universal, Sameness.

We breathe out what we call *breath*, and more than that, we add our specific voice, in specific tones, through a specific throat, at a specific time: form, the unique individual, Difference.

And as we chant, we can realize that we're a perfect union of the unique and the universal, a harmony of Difference and Sameness.

Of course, it's very appropriate to practice chanting as part of our work studying a song, right? Chanting helps us to memorize material, which is helpful. But the remembering is more of the body than of the brain. We remember our multiplication tables with our brains through simple repetition. But we seem to remember song lyrics in a different way.

Chanting something—as opposed to simply reading or reciting it—creates an intimacy with the chanted. It's more than an intellectual reviewing of the content (although that happens). It's hearing and feeling the piece coming out of your own body, sounds created by your own mouth and lips, coming from deep within your own body. It's the shape of the sounds, the rounding of the mouth, the attention to the pitch and pace, the careful spaces and breaths.

The carefulness that chanting demands helps us to connect to the words so closely that sometimes the connection disappears and there's just one thing happening. We grow into a kind of ownership with what we chant. It sometimes feels like the words are part of us and are coming from inside us, like something we've always known, always been, from even before we were born.

There's a vast difference between this perception:

> Some old Zen guy wrote that his body and mind were the Buddha.

and this one:

> the sound of *"This very body, the Buddha"* coming out of your body, your lungs, your mouth, in your voice, and in real time.

When we chant this verse ourselves, it's pretty hard to think that *this very body, the Buddha* applies to anyone other than us.

REMEMBER WHAT YOU ARE

"You're perfect the way you are. And you could use a little improvement."

What's the improvement part? Why do we need improvement?

Because we misunderstand. And because we misunderstand, we suffer. We suffer and we cause others to suffer.

But our misunderstanding doesn't change what's fundamental. We are tigers raised as goats, as the old Sufi story goes, and when we remember what we are, our lives change. But we were tigers all the while.

I read recently that tigers have striped skin, not just striped fur. And the stripes are unique, like our fingerprints—no two tigers have the same pattern.

The tiger-ness of tigers is tattooed into their DNA and is written in calligraphy on their skin. Even a shaved tiger would still be a tiger.

Hakuin is starting this Song with the most fundamental truth, that despite our very real greed, hate, and delusion, Buddha is our DNA. Awakeness is our nature.

3

H O W   S A D

How sad that people ignore the near
And search for truth afar:
Like someone in the midst of water
Crying out in thirst,
Like a child of a wealthy home
Wandering among the poor.

How sad. Sadness. Yes. The state of the world, the state of the human heart so much of the time. A defining experience of life.

Buddhism starts with the recognition of the universality of the experience of suffering. We call it the First Noble Truth. It's a brave and honest place for a religion to start, and I love it for that.

This stanza's reference to feeling lost and despairing is especially pertinent in meditation settings. The Song was written by a monk and likely intended for other monks. These folks spend their lives in monasteries, far from the madding crowds, and they do lots (*lots*) of meditation.

If we're new to these things, we can imagine that they lived in some sort of paradise: *Wow, those temples and monasteries are so peaceful! I wish I lived at one! Then I could really still my mind and find some peace. Those nuns and monks are so lucky, living such a simple, ideal life. No wonder they're so content all the time!*

Sound familiar? If that was actually the case, you'd think Hakuin would've skipped the sad, thirsty, lost, dark stuff. But he didn't.

And if we're honest, the sad, thirsty, lost dark stuff is why we're all here, thinking about Zen and the nature of life. Once, during a koan workshop that Norman Fischer was leading at Minnesota Zen Center, he said, "We have religion because we die."

I agree. It feels right to me that religion (or spirituality; I'm not separating those two right now) arises from a deep impulse to search for meaning and explanations about the very nature of our lives. And that deep impulse would seem to arise in us because we know something that no other life form on this planet seems to: *We are all going to die.* That primary realization causes us untold difficulty and struggle.

FEARING SEPARATENESS

Underlying the fear of death is the assumption of separation—that we're separate beings that are born and die. We believe we're separate, so death scares us because we fear not-being, obliteration, annihilation. If we didn't imagine ourselves to be separate, we'd see birth and death in a very different way.

When we're sitting down, we have a nice lap. When we stand, it disappears. We don't think of our lap as having died; we know that our legs just changed shape. How do you tell your lap not to be scared, that when you stand up it really doesn't end, it just changes? How do you tell your fist not to be scared when you're about to open your hand?

But whether the belief is a misunderstanding or not, the fear is a very real. Horribly, horribly real.

We call our reaction to this fear *suffering*, and it's an intimate acquaintance of all of us. To intimately know my own suffering is therefore to know much about yours. Our universal experience of suffering can give birth to a brilliant response in the human: empathy, and sometimes, compassion. Seeing your pain can pluck a similar string in my heart, as I know at least some version of what you're feeling. I feel closer to you in those moments because we feel less separate.

Perhaps this is why we feel more intimacy with others at an Alcoholics Anonymous meeting than at a book club or the PTA.

Because of compassion, we get a tiny glimpse into the reality of our non-separateness. We see through the illusion of separation and we are mutually healed by that experience.

And of course, we immediately forget after a moment of connection and we go back to autopilot, believing in our terminal separateness.

That's part of why we practice zazen so much in the Zen tradition. Both the compassion and the inclusive spaciousness we can experience help us to drop the illusion of our separateness—and the more we do it the better we get at it.

DIAGNOSING OUR SUFFERING

So, Buddhism really does start with suffering because it's the most honest and logical point to start. If we lived forever and life didn't hurt, we wouldn't have much incentive to ask the big questions: they wouldn't exist.

The Four Noble Truths follow the medical model we still use:

1. Diagnosis
2. Cause
3. Prognosis
4. Cure

It's a pattern that's familiar to all of us. We go to the doctor because we have a rash on our leg, and she says, "Oh, this is poison ivy. Have you been wearing shorts in the woods lately? You'll be fine, just apply this cream twice a day for a week." She just diagnosed our problem (poison ivy), told us the cause (exposure to poison ivy on bare skin), gave a prognosis (you'll be fine), and offered us a cure (the cream) and instructions to use it. Pretty simple.

The Buddha did the same thing for the human species. He noticed that:

1) Human life is characterized by *dukkha*.

Dukkha is a Sanskrit term that refers to suffering, lack of ease, discontentment, discord, struggle, angst, etc. Dukkha has the same root as the word used in Sanskrit to describe a wagon wheel that is off-center. The wheel might work, but something isn't right. It's important to know that dukkha refers to a wide spectrum of experience, from obvious and gross forms of suffering all the way to very subtle, itch-on-the-back-of-the-neck types of vague discontent. Very, very few of our moments, if any, do not contain at least a subtle hint of dukkha.

2) We suffer because we want what we do not have and have what we do not want.

We resist reality as it is. We defend against it. We wish it were other than it is. (When I teach this, I sometimes use the acronym WITBO—"Wishing It To Be Otherwise"—to help people remember this simple idea.) And the harder we resist reality and the more we wish it were different, the more we suffer.

3) But the prognosis is good, as the human heart-mind is trainable and more capable than we normally think. "There is an end to suffering," the Buddha taught, "because I have ended it in myself and you can too."

4) And he offered a remedy to help us work with the condition of suffering, the Eightfold Noble Path (see the Appendix for a brief overview).

WE CAN'T SEE THAT WE'RE ALREADY HOME

How sad that people ignore the near
And search for truth afar

We know this teaching; we've heard this kind of thing before: "She looked and looked and then discovered that it was hers all along." Or as the Good Witch of the East says to Dorothy in Oz, "You've always had the power to go home."

We see echoes of this idea all over, from literature to spiritual metaphor to common sayings, all saying that the path is not a straight line but a circle. They all seem to agree that we do have to leave in order to return and see what our lives really are, to know "them for the first time," as T. S. Eliot says at the end of his *Four Quartets*.

While the Song opened with *all beings*, now, in the second stanza, *people*—that is to say, human beings—arrive. We're the ones who ignore the near and get lost, we're the ones who misunderstand and suffer. We're also nature's masterpiece. We're the ones living on this blue marble who have the highest potential for good, for compassion, for awakening. We're the heart of this world, and if it's to survive, we're the ones who must see its wounds and ours, feel its pain and ours, and do something loving to save both it and ourselves. In short, we are uniquely able to love. And despite our tremendous capacity for delusion and causing destruction, we are also the pinnacles of evolution, the only hope.

"You have gained the pivotal opportunity of human form," Buddhist scripture says. The question is what you'll choose to do with it.

Yet we ignore the near and search for truth afar.

> His disciples said to him, "When is the kingdom going to come?"
>
> Jesus said, "It is not by being waited for that it is going to come. They are not going to say, 'Here it is' or 'There it is.' Rather, the kingdom of the Father is spread out over the earth, and people do not see it."
>
> —*The Gospel of Thomas, logion #113*

So here's this same teaching idea again, telling us we were actually home all the time that we were so fervently searching for our home.

But how real is this idea to us when our pain, our suffering is very real? When the lost pet, the broken heart, the cancer diagnosis is all too real? When we're that thirsty, we lose sight of our water nature that Hakuin tells us is all around.

We like the idea of this teaching, and may even claim to believe it, but when things become difficult for us, the idea and belief are of little comfort. Regardless of what belief or lofty spiritual idea is in our heads, we trust our actual felt experience: *I hurt.*

Can we be present to *I hurt* in a way that sees it, accepts it, asks after it, holds it with kindness?

Can we trust that *I hurt* is included in enlightenment?

That's what zazen is: a Buddha space of unlimited and unconditional wisdom, acceptance, courage, compassion. Zazen is the gate to a thousand Dharmaverses, the opening to see this reality, including its *I hurt*, as complete, whole, lacking nothing, wanting nothing to be different.

FEEL YOUR THIRST SO THAT
YOU CAN FEEL OTHERS'

Like someone in the midst of water crying out in thirst. My emotional response to Hakuin's image of the thirsty person is compassion for their suffering, then a longing for them to find the wisdom that helps them see that they are surrounded by what they need. We all know thirst, and we can all see the tragedy of being thirsty while surrounded by water. The universal metaphor of thirst seems perfectly offered to create compassion and wisdom in the mind and heart of the reader.

It's important that we understand these qualities and the order in which they most helpfully arise. Compassion first. Wisdom second. And compassion arises from sadness. We skip sadness at our peril.

Without compassion, wisdom is a cold examining room table, a ruthless law, a reckless sword. Explain to a crying baby precisely why he or she is uncomfortable or explain to a feral cat why she needn't fear you and should take the food from your hand.

Wisdom without compassion isn't really wisdom. It's dry soup mix in a waterless desert, an empty house, a legal arrangement between no one and no one. Of course, compassion without wisdom also isn't compassion; it's codependency, enmeshment, and enabling.

But what I see most often, especially in spiritual circles, is people rushing to get to the wisdom bit and ignoring or skipping over the compassion bit.

And of course they do. Compassion hurts, and we don't like to hurt. In fact, most of us drawn to a disciplined spiritual path are drawn to it—consciously or unconsciously—to get away from the pain of our lives. We want enlightenment because we imagine it's a place filled with love that never hurts, a perfect wave that crests but never breaks.

And here is the water metaphor again, the metaphor for our truest nature, being used to describe that which we are and that which surrounds us, yet that which we thirst for. *In the midst of water, crying out in thirst.*

The likening of the spiritual impulse to thirst is one that touches me deeply. I'm a recovering alcoholic and I long mistook whiskey for the holy.

After some years of sobriety, I heard a woman at my weekly AA meeting say, "I think my drinking was a misguided attempt at a spiritual experience," and I was floored. What she said made perfect sense to me, and I knew it had been true for me too.

Years ago, I worked at a liquor store, which is rather obviously a bad place for an alcoholic to work. But I did anyway. I was often scheduled for the opening shift, and so I was the one to unlock the doors and wait on the first customers of the day. We had a regular customer who, the six days a week that we were open, was always the first in the door. And he always bought the same thing, a 750 of Philips Vodka. (Except on Saturdays, when he'd buy a larger bottle because liquor stores are closed on Sundays in Minnesota and he had to plan ahead.)

He always paid with a check, always the exact same amount, right to the penny. And I always made him follow the stupid store policy and write his phone number on the memo line, even though his checks never bounced and he had the same phone number as the day before. I was consistently, passively, and pointlessly mean to him because I was disgusted by him. I wanted to make it just a little harder for him because I disliked him so much: I was repelled by his chalky, too-pale skin, his red eyes, his sloppy yet robotic movements, his shaking hands. He always wanted a slim paper bag to put his bottle in, and I never offered it—I always made him ask. I hated that he was trying to hide his alcoholism. I wanted to world to know, and I wanted him to feel ashamed.

I know now that he was a man in the grip of a deep addiction who had terrific suffering. He wasn't living, he was dying.

I know this because I had the same illness that he did, but I didn't know it yet. He was my future. A few short months after I lost that exact job, I too was asking for my bottles in paper bags and paying for them with poorly written checks. The only difference was that my checks often bounced. His never did.

When I replay my memories of him, my heart gets heavy and slow. I feel ashamed. And I want to hate my past self. How easy that would be.

But hating my past self helps nothing and changes nothing. What does help is to understand who I was, what I felt, and why I did what I did. The truth is, I was scared of him.

Underneath my self-satisfied disgust, I was scared of his world, of his obvious suffering. So I made an unconscious and almost immediate choice to cover that fear with anger, with revulsion. I chose not to feel his suffering because I imagined that it wasn't mine. I imagined that his life and my life were not connected. I imagined that we were separate.

I was wrong.

My practice now is to see my mistake, and to understand why I did what I did. I see, then accept, then forgive my own unconsciousness, my own fear. I explore and feel fully. My old self doesn't need to be blamed, shamed, or punished any more than that man did. Blame, shame, and punishment don't help. They make things worse.

My practice now is to let my heart break for who I was and to hold that pain in my own loving awareness. My practice now is to go back and feel what I felt: my anger, and under it, my fear, and under that, my shame, to let my heart break for myself and hold myself while it happens. I am the thirster and the drinker; I am the holder, and I am the held. This is healing for me.

My practice now is to let my heart break for him, that lost shell of a human, that being who was in such tremendous pain that the hazy gray oblivion of drunkenness was the only way to make life bearable. This is healing for my relationship with what I imagine to be "other." When we arrive at the honest and undiluted awareness of others' suffering, compassion awakens naturally in us.

THE FIRE OF COMPASSION

Compassion is the highest ideal and holiest practice of Zen Buddhism. Hakuin, if he's the person we imagine him to be, must've been describing actual, real compassion and not clean empathy, polite sympathy, or the sickness of pity.

But when I first started chanting the Song of Zazen, I took Hakuin's words in this stanza as pity at worst and perhaps sympathy at best. I think of pity as, "Oh, you poor thing," actually meaning, "keep away." It's a distancing tactic, and it's a superior position. Perhaps you've been on the receiving end of pity. It's disgusting.

Sympathy seems like one level better; it's more like an "I'm using my imagination to put myself in your shoes, and it's probably bad" kind of thing. To receive sympathy isn't too bad, but it doesn't usually help us much either, as there's still a lot of distance there.

Then we come to empathy, which is far too rare, but is a huge step up from sympathy. It involves feeling something of what they must feel, often by remembering something in our own experience that was similar. In other words, empathy is starting to actually *feel with*, not just *think about* the other. Empathizing with someone is the beginning of compassion.

Finally, we get to compassion, and that's the hardest and rarest thing.

Compassion is a very fashionable word these days in spiritual circles, but it's largely misunderstood. We usually think compassion is a nice, gooey, saccharine emotion, but it's not. The awakening of real compassion can burn like fire.

To be inside another's suffering and to take it on as our own—and yet not lose ourselves in it—is the highest practice, the expression of the deepest understanding. Tibetan Buddhists call this practice *ton-glen.* Compassion is literally "to suffer with," and it can hurt terribly. *Do it anyway. It's your own life you're feeling. Don't turn it off.*

GO DOWN DEEP

In his commencement speech at Spelman College in May, 1980, Howard Thurman, the brilliant Christian theologian, civil rights activist, and spiritual director to Dr. Martin Luther King, Jr., said:

> I can become quiet enough, still enough, to hear the sound of the genuine in me. I can become quiet enough, still enough, to hear the sound of the genuine in you. Now if I hear the sound of the genuine in me, and if you hear the sound of the genuine in you, it is possible for me to go down in me and come up in you. So that when I look at myself through your eyes having made that pilgrimage, I see in me what you see in me and the wall that separates and divides will disappear and we will become one because the sound of the genuine makes the same music.

Suffering is genuine. So is love, hope, longing, and joy. When we're intimate with what's most fundamental about our own personal life, we become intimate with what's most fundamental about everyone else's. The particle understands itself as the wave and vice versa. Go down into your own suffering all the way. Then you find the suffering of others. Then you will find love.

If you want to further explore the dynamic relationship with suffering in your own meditation, try this during your zazen:

Settle into your posture and take few minutes to allow the top layer of mind-dust (busy thinking, restless body, etc.) to settle.

Then, when you're feeling a bit more centered and able to be present to your inner world, on your inhalation, move your awareness down inside your body and emotions. Rest it there and breathe until you notice a constriction or a particular suffering. That might be nervousness about an upcoming event, an uncomfortable memory, or even a reluctance to do this exercise. Then, on your next exhalation, try to release the specific narrative around your suffering (the story) and see if you can relax into simply being a loving witness to your suffering. Rest there and breathe. Watch the story reassert itself, and then release it gently on the exhalation. Inhale back into simple, loving presence to the body and emotion, *the actual experience of the suffering itself.*

Over time, you will start becoming aware of the dynamic of resistance and then surrender, over and over again. We fear our suffering and offer resistance; then we surrender and move into it with grace and increasing ease. If you remain a distant and aloof (i.e., unfeeling) witness, you are stuck. If you remain identified with the suffering (i.e., losing the loving witness) you are stuck. Notice that the more fluid and graceful this flowing dynamic is, the more you expand into more lightness, freedom, and joy.

THE CLOUDS AND THE RIVER ARE NOT TWO

Show me a drop of water that doesn't have lake nature. The drop contains the lake, not the other way around.

But we don't see or understand ourselves as made of the same stuff as Buddha, that our minds are, in essence, the same as enlightened minds. So we look elsewhere, we look outside. We look to teachers, teachings, to the future, to the past, to elsewhere. We search outside ourselves, and we look far away.

Dogen says it this way:

> *If you follow the river all the way back to its source, there are the clouds.*
> *If you follow the clouds all the way back to their source, there is the river.*
> *This means "no source."*

Source outside ourselves we call *infinity*. Source inside ourselves we call *self*.

Breath outside our body we call *air*. Air inside our body we call *breath*. One is impersonal and unseen, one is life itself. And they are not two separate things.

There's a koan in Zen that talks about teaching penetrating the "skin, flesh, bones, and marrow." We think this is about progress and stages and going from shallow to deep, from bad to good. We think a butterfly is better—or at least further along—than a caterpillar. And in a sense, it is, but that sense is pretty linear and pretty limited. Is a five-year-old kid just an incomplete adult? Of course not. They're already complete in their five-year-old-ness.

But think about air and breath; think about skin and marrow. What's best? Who wins?

There are not separate things. The river is the clouds and the clouds are the river and there are two things and there are not two things. The skin is the marrow, the marrow is the skin.

SEEK, AND YOU ARE FAR AWAY

How close are you to you? How close are you to Source?

Closer than your breath, closer than your thoughts, closer than all your ideas of "close."

How close are you to Source? isn't even the right question because even the word *close* implies space, and Source knows nothing of space. Or time, for that matter, or limits of any kind.

But our limitlessness shows itself to us in its apparent limits: time, space, skin, flesh, bones, marrow. Our form is how we know consciousness. Our consciousness is how we know form.

The building blocks of creation urge us to look into and through them, like the bars on a cage at the zoo urge us to see through them to the animal beyond. Like black letters on a page urge us to see the idea, the story, the feeling for being alive that lies beyond them.

We don't go to the zoo to see cages, and we don't read to see words.

We do both to have an experience of being alive. That's where God lies—in our experience. What else do we know but our experience? Where else could Source reside?

Words like *skin, flesh, bones*, and *marrow* are just ways of talking about our experience of being alive in form. It's all we know. Our skin isn't closer to us than our marrow. It's not a stepladder of intimacy—the intimacy is complete, unbounded, and total, in every moment.

Our ideas of "past" come up in our sittings and in our lives because we think we live there—those memories are our sense of self. And our ideas of "future" come up in our sittings because we imagine that's the place we're going that can save us—that's where things will change and we'll finally arrive at contentment and joy. But neither is ultimately true—no past and no future means no self and no salvation or contentment beyond *this.*

Where is God, truth, you? Where is your real life, your vast, inconceivable Source?

Seek and you are far away. Instead, align your skin, flesh, bones, and marrow into the shape of stability, dignity, equanimity, contentment, and then past, future, and present can merge on their own.

When you're gone, the universe isn't missing a "you." The completeness of creation doesn't include or exclude you.

If you follow yourself all the way back to your source, there is all Creation. If you follow all Creation all the way back to its source, there is you. Creation wasn't incomplete before your birth nor will it be less complete after you die. Birth doesn't add nor does death subtract.

Where did you come from? Here, now!

Where will you go? Here, now!

There is nowhere else to go.

4

LOST

Lost on dark paths of ignorance,
We wander through the Six Worlds,
From dark path to dark path—
When shall we be freed from birth and death?

Lost on dark paths of ignorance.... This is despair, an almost existential place for us as humans. This is when life shows up as hopeless suffering with no end. This is a dark place from which we cry out: *When shall we be freed from birth and death?*

Sometimes when I chant this line, my voice comes out light and unburdened. Maybe I'm in a good place and I'm not too troubled because life seems okay just then, and plus, I know what's coming next: *Oh, the zazen of the Mahayana ...*

But sometimes when I chant this line, my voice comes out quiet, or gritty, or choked with emotion. Like many of us, I know this dark place well. Some of us are more familiar with the periods of darkness than the periods of light that can follow. I'm usually quicker to believe the bad news than the good, and despair can feel truer than hope and ideas of freedom.

We can all identify with the feelings Hakuin is alluding to here: searching, being lost, frightened, frustrated, despairing.

Where will I find relief? Peace? Comfort? Freedom?

Will I find it in financial security, respect in my field, my family, staying busy? Mindfulness, religion, spirituality, meditation? What combination will best fill my void and numb my pain?

Which of those will become dark paths for me, leading nowhere, and which might offer me some of the feeling of connection and intimacy I long for?

THE REALMS OF AFFLICTION

We all know how pervasive depression and anxiety are in the world. We all know that, despite many cultures' increased standard of living and technological comforts, we are no closer to inner peace as a species than we were when Hakuin taught, or the Buddha.

Hakuin would surely have recognized this state intimately as a place he'd been—a place we all visit—many times; *we wander through the Six Realms.*

Despite their metaphysical-sounding names, the Six Realms (or Six Worlds) are simply a Buddhist psychological model of the states of being that we all inhabit from day to day. They are:

1. The Hell Realm, where suffering is intense and horrible
2. The Hungry Ghost Realm, where we only experience insatiable longing
3. The Fighting Realm, where we can only experience conflict
4. The Heaven Realm, where we're too distracted with idle comfort to have self-awareness, do our practice, or care about others
5. The Animal Realm, where we're identified with only our basest natures
6. The Human Realm, where we are when we're not too caught by the other five less-desirable ones

All six realms contain suffering, although some contain more than others. For example, the Hell Realm has too much suffering for us to do much practice, and the Heaven Realm has too little. And since practice is what actually transforms suffering and frees beings, even Heaven isn't desirable—the Heaven Realm is where compassion goes to die. So the desirable realm to occupy is actually where we already are: the Human Realm. That's where our suffering is present enough to motivate us and connect us to others, but where we're not overwhelmed by the power of the suffering or distraction of the other five Realms. Sometimes the Realms are illustrated as a five-petaled flower with the Human Realm at the center, the place you want to be.

In describing the dark paths of ignorance, Hakuin is saying that to not know the truth is *dukkha*, suffering. And we can never know all of the truth, so there's always some *dukkha* sniffing around our feet. But that's the human experience, so we don't need to worry about it. Worrying about it would create more *dukkha*, right?

But describing the affliction is important. Knowing how we're feeling in any given moment is important. Having words to express those feelings is important. Words have power, and they can be used to not only empower and reify our emotions, but also to help to connect us to others.

In the Song, Hakuin uses several words to describe different forms of suffering: *sad, thirsty, poor, lost, dark, ignorant,* and *enslaved* or *imprisoned* (implied by *when shall we be freed?*).

Zen Buddhism has a slightly different take on suffering than traditional Buddhism does. In Zen, as I understand it, suffering is less of an enemy to be vanquished or extinguished and more of a powerful and pervasive field of fertile soil in which to plant the seeds of compassion. One practical way of doing this is to play with words a bit. The next time you notice the arising of an afflictive emotional state like loneliness, anger, or grief, say to yourself, "Oh, I am experiencing the loneliness," instead of "I am lonely" or "This loneliness is mine."

See if doing this changes your experience at all. With some practice, it may help you stay in the role of the compassionate observer (Buddha), and not identify yourself so strongly with the suffering that you're experiencing.

SUFFERING IS OUR ALLY AND TEACHER

My suffering isn't just "mine." It also just *is*. It's The Suffering, and we all take turns feeling it. It comes, it changes, it goes. And that can actually be okay. We can actually be okay—deeply okay, and even content—in the midst of great pain if we don't own it, grasp it, defend against it, or resist it. Suffering melts into pain, and pain sucks but it is really just energy that's telling us something. It's an ally, not an enemy.

All of our emotions are holy messengers. They faithfully give us vital and important information about this All, both about our specific experience of it and our connection to it.

More than we long for comfort, we long for the feeling of being authentically alive. More than pleasure, we long for deep, authentic connection to others. Knowing what it is to be heartbroken allows you to really inhabit sitting with your heartbroken friend.

Rumi talks about this cry for freedom and connection in a poem that Coleman Barks translated and called "Love Dogs." Here's part of it:

> *The grief you cry out from*
> *draws you toward union.*
> *Your pure sadness*
> *that wants help*
> *is the secret cup.*
> *Listen to the moan of a dog for its master.*
> *That whining is the connection.*
> *There are love dogs*
> *no one knows the names of.*
> *Give your life*
> *to be one of them.*

This is a difficult teaching. We can use that difficulty to help us though, by seeing it as a barometer for our practice: our ability to hold it and feel its truth gives a clear glimpse of our limitations.

Suffering is not a foe to defeat, it's a teacher to learn from.

HEROES OF COMPASSION

My first hero was Harriet Tubman. I read a book about her when I was in grade school and was astounded by her clarity, strength, and almost inhuman courage. Her initial escape from slavery and her harrowing journey to the Mason-Dixon line was, for her, precisely, and only, the beginning. Her freedom wasn't just for her and it wasn't attained when she found herself in the North.

Once she discovered that there was a path to freedom, that it was possible, she went right back down again. Why? Because she knew that she wasn't free yet because others were still slaves. In that way, Harriet Tubman acted just like what a Zen Buddhist might call a *bodhisattva.*

The bodhisattva ideal of compassion moved me all those years ago, and it still moves me now. The bodhisattva is one who practices for the sake of enlightenment, like everyone does, but enlightenment to better serve, support, and enlighten others. It's like learning to swim to eventually become a lifeguard. The idea is that a bodhisattva—literally an "enlightening being"—is so moved by compassion for all suffering beings (i.e., all beings), that on the threshold of complete and final Nirvana, they turn back to the suffering world, again and again over countless trillions of lives, until everyone is saved, until everyone is free. "I will practice until all the hells are empty," says the bodhisattva, and although in this cosmology everyone—everything—eventually attains complete perfect enlightened Buddhahood, the Bodhisattva will be the last one through the door.

I think we can all identify this energy in ourselves. It's the parent who won't sleep until all the kids are safe home in bed, it's the heaviness you feel in your heart when you know a loved one is in pain, it's the firefighter who's the last one out of the burning home, carrying a scared kitten.

MEETING SUFFERING WITH KINDNESS

In Zen Buddhism, we have Jizo Bodhisattva. He/she/it/they (bodhisattvas can show up in whatever form is most helpful) is a being so devoted to freeing all beings from suffering that they have the unique ability to gain access to the many hells where people find themselves. Jizo is sometimes depicted as wearing robes that are singed at the bottom, burned from the many fires. Jizo vows not to stop practicing until all the hells are empty.

And we admire Jizo, we love Jizo. But we don't want to *be* Jizo.

And yet this is exactly what must be done. We must be Jizo and we must start by being Jizo for ourselves. Meditation and spiritual or religious practice are too often used as an escape, an attempt to bypass the real work of transforming human suffering and making lofty ideals like love, compassion, and equanimity *real*.

Jizo is all about roll-up-your-sleeves-and-do-the-dirty-work.

To do this, we do lots of reminding ourselves of our highest intentions while holding our pain and humanness with great patience, care, and understanding.

If it hurts, it's saying something. Pain is message, suffering is intimate communion with our past. We must tend to it as we would a crying infant.

So we try and try, with lots of gentleness, like when we were learning to walk or tie our shoes. It's so hard! It takes such time!

Of course it does! No problem. Nothing is wrong with us; we're just learning to do something new that's very difficult.

One of the gifts of zazen (when understood and practiced properly) is that it shows us our defenses against suffering, then peels them back and shows us the underlying pain, allowing us to actually meet it with compassion, to feel it with acceptance and *metta* (kindness, love).

This is actually healing a core wound, whereas simply addressing or suppressing symptoms (through distractions, avoidance, suppression, dissociating, spiritual bypass, drink and drugs, etc.), although palliative, isn't correctional or therapeutic. We don't heal, we just stop feeling the pain.

At some point in sincere practice, the top layer of chatter starts to peel back. Either that, or we start sensing what that top layer is connected to underneath. We start to see, then to feel, the human condition: our condition. We come face to face, then heart to heart, with the sad, thirsty, lost darkness. And it is not an obstacle to overcome. It is not a demon to be vanquished, a dragon to be killed, a noise to be silenced, a foe to escape from, a pain to be transcended.

Because the suffering we find is literally us. When you find anger in you, it's yours. It's you finding a part of you. And, most importantly, it's you finding a suffering part of you.

How you meet your own suffering says a lot about you and your practice.

Will you ignore your suffering, as you might ignore an irritating crying baby?

Will you distract yourself from it, using a YouTube video or a nice mantra?

Will you shut it off with a strong drink, drug, or daydream?

Will you just stick with "understanding" your suffering by explaining its nature and origins and leave it at that?

Will you judge your suffering to be illogical, unwarranted, unnecessary, or unworthy of you?

Will you "transcend" that suffering by losing yourself in lofty realms of meditative absorption?

THE TEMPTATION OF TRANSCENDENCE

Wounds are not healed by ignoring them, denying them, suppressing them, scolding them, distracting ourselves from them, or trying to explain them away.

And we see this all the time in spiritual communities of all kinds. We see people completely devoted to great paths of awakening, beauty, and love who, after years of practice, are still angry, scattered, selfish, lost. Why?

They're using their prayer or meditation time as an escape. They're spacing out, dissociating, daydreaming. They feel great on the cushion—calm and peaceful—and mostly crappy off of it. They haven't been taught correctly, so they still have no sense of what's alive within them, no sense of the ocean of human suffering of which they are a part, and no sense of what to skillfully do with their suffering when it arises.

A two-word instruction can change this. When you notice suffering, *Love it.*

Simple to say, hard to do.

Hard because most often, we're stuck in those Six Realms.

Compassion literally means to be with suffering, and we all know that suffering is not an easy feather bed to be in. It's so hard to be with suffering, in fact, that we rarely are. We suffer all the time, of course, and we're exposed to the suffering of others all the time too. But we're almost never *just with it.*

Why? Because it's really hard. We often don't feel that we're strong enough, that we don't have the capacity, that we just can't take it. So we try as hard as we can to not feel it.

OUR DEFENSES ARE PROTECTORS, BUT WE DON'T ALWAYS STILL NEED THEM

When Hakuin says, "From dark path to dark path...." I often think of our fight/flight/freeze defenses. We toggle back and forth between them, and despite their circumstantial usefulness (especially when we're very young), they are all ultimately dark, dead-end paths in that they don't allow for growth and evolution. They can, and usually do, keep us stuck.

Our barriers and defenses against suffering are well-practiced habits, and for most of us, those walls are thick and high. We find and create defenses against suffering when we're very young because we have to in order to survive.

An easy example of this might be the playground bully. The bully intimidates and hurts others as a way to prove their strength and power. Why? Well, everyone who's taken Psych 101 knows that—they feel weak and powerless inside. Their bullying is a tactic to (a) help them feel strong and powerful and (b) distance themselves from their core wound, their core belief that they are weak and powerless (which is to say, ashamed).

As adults, we forget how vulnerable we are when we're young. We forget that our physical survival depended completely on adults. When those adults give you the message to be a certain way to keep them happy, you do it. When they give you the message to not do something that pisses them off, you stop.

Even the most thickheaded, reckless skydivers take very, very good care of their parachutes. Because if one thing goes wrong, it's game over. Same with us—all of us—when we were little kids. Those adults were the parachute, and you just don't mess with that.

The defenses we employed were more than clever, more than adaptive, more than skillful—they were brilliant. They enabled us to stay alive.

When I hear people badmouth their egos, their defenses, and their "delusions," it feels like I'm listening to someone who survived a shipwreck, made it to shore, and then turns and badmouths the lifeboat that got them there.

Of course we want to go past the simple functioning of the ego and to integrate its useful functioning. If we're really fortunate, at some point we see the downside to the ego's defenses and the limits of its agenda. We see how it begins to create more suffering than it protects us from. But to really see this is not to see an enemy to defeat—*the horrible devil called ego*—but to recognize with wonder and gratitude the functioning that kept us alive. If we're paying attention, we understand why those walls were so important: the threats that necessitated them were real.

And now, even as somewhat adaptive adults, those old walls are still trying to keep us insulated and safe. But they don't anymore, of course. Nor are they necessary any longer. They just keep us isolated from the truth, from each other, and from ourselves. Numb. Dead.

And so we need practice at climbing those walls. We need to strengthen our compassion muscles, to increase our holding potential.

COMPASSION AND BOUNDARIES

When I was living in downtown Minneapolis years ago, my friend Ben turned me on to a great green tea that I could buy in bulk at a local Asian grocery where I also bought my mock duck. The tea was called Temple of Heaven Gunpowder, and it was cheap, and it had a smoky taste I loved. It was also good cold, so I drank it like water during the summer and I half-pretended that it had magical qualities. (Okay, full-pretended.)

I've since learned that Temple of Heaven Gunpowder is widely and easily available, but for me at that time, it felt like finding the Ark of the Covenant.

Years later, a tea-loving friend with a more refined palette than mine bought me five ounces of Iron Goddess of Mercy Oolong, which I decided I loved before I even tried it—the name alone was reason enough to drink it.

It was delicious and lent itself to multiple steepings. It was more expensive but was also good served cold during the summer. So one summer I decided to mix the cheap tea with the more expensive one, and I created my own hybrid that I call the Iron Goddess of Gunpowder.

It's brilliant.

Talking about compassion and mercy in the same breath as iron and gunpowder sounds funny, and it can be. But one of the most common misunderstandings about compassion is that it's a weak, powerless state of boundarylessness. It's being a pushover, a doormat, a feather bed—a victim.

Wrong. Compassion isn't like that.

The goddess of compassion (called Avalokiteshvara, Kwan Yin, Kanzeon, among other names) has a thousand gentle arms and tear-filled eyes and infinite soft beds to help us into when we need that. She also has teeth and iron and gunpowder when she needs to, and she uses them without delay because her compassion is tempered with the clarity of wisdom. Love is always wise. So she knows where the boundaries must be drawn, and she draws them and she enforces them.

In spiritual communities, we often equate loose or nonexistent boundaries with being loving or compassionate. Wrong. Compassion is no weakling, and love will throw us around the room if it needs to, to try and get our attention. The voice of compassion can come out as, "I'd be happy to help," or, "I am so sorry that you're in pain," or, "No, thanks; I'm not interested" or even, "You're hurting me. Back off." We need the iron and gunpowder side of compassion.

I have struggled mightily with this teaching in my life. I have long associated kindness and love only with gentleness and softness, and of course it can, and should, show up that way. But it was harder for me to accept the iron and gunpowder as love too. When I was ignored, I just went with it, trying to convince myself that I could embrace being unseen as a kind of humble anonymity. When I was insulted, I said nothing, trying to convince myself that I was being long-fused and patient. When I was trespassed against or violated in some way, I tried to frame my nonresistance as forgiveness, radical acceptance, or transcendent wisdom.

But the truth is that I was not humble, patient, forgiving, or wise. I felt sad, hurt, angry, and resentful. And my denying the truth of that pain wasn't helpful or loving to me or to my perpetrators. It wasn't true. It wasn't relational. It offered no hope of connection or insight. It wasn't love.

It was the withdrawal that often accompanies fear, plain and simple. I was scared, so I shut down. And since I'm a "spiritual" person,

I reframed my flight defense as patience, acceptance, wisdom—blah, blah, blah.

Maybe that's why the Goddess of Mercy is made of iron. She's no weakling. If she were made of straw or wood, she might not be strong enough to hold your pain. Maybe that's why we need gunpowder from time to time, because power, when used in the service of wisdom, compassion, and the principles of non-harm, becomes something more than just crude force. It becomes a generative energy that frees beings from suffering. The power of practice helps us lower those ancient walls and let in some air, let in some light. That's the power, the magic gunpowder, of zazen. We can find our way free from birth and death.

When? Hakuin asks. Now.

5

THE HIGHEST PRAISE

Oh, the zazen of the Mahayana!
To this the highest praise!
Devotion, repentance, training,
The many paramitas—
All have their source in zazen.

A common misunderstanding about meditation—zazen in particular—is that it's designed to either (a) stop your thinking entirely, or (b) help you create a lovely mindspace that's all about serenity, all about blissing out, all about escape.

But if you're looking to escape from the experience of your actual life, I wouldn't recommend zazen, because your life is all that zazen offers you.

Zazen is just another name for awareness practice. It is the opposite of escape. It's direct experience of our actual life. And this direct experience includes all of Mind: brain, body, and emotions.

This radical inclusivity of all experience is what makes zazen both wisdom practice and compassion practice. Our awareness is intended to be full awareness, and when we catch ourselves wandering, we've just included our wandering in our awareness—so we've just returned.

Hakuin is saying that everything in a life of awakening has its source in zazen, but here he focuses on devotion, repentance, and training—in short, the entire life of an ordained Zen Buddhist nun or monk, Hakuin's audience.

Hakuin is inviting us to see both repentance and devotion as expressions of zazen, as natural extensions of our ongoing self-awareness practice. And therefore to see zazen as an expression of devotion and repentance. How often do we think of our daily zazen as devotional? How often do we see it as repentance?

THE EVERYDAY SACRED

Do we have devotional practice in Zen? Oh, yes. In fact, one way of viewing practice is that it is nothing but devotion.

My teacher goes by one of his birth names, Tim. It's from the Greek word *timotheos*, which means "to honor God." When he asked his Roman Catholic grandmother about God and how to honor Him, she said, "Just worship the God in front of you."

The heart of devotion we cultivate in Zen is devoted to what's in front of us. Right here, right now. That's the sacred thing, the sacred moment—whatever is here. No picking and choosing, just say yes.

We say our practice should be wholehearted, which means we don't leave anything out of it. We respond to the God in front of us with a whole heart, not a part. After a while we get a feel for this and can even feel when we're only offering part of ourselves, when we're holding something back.

"There is no place to spit" is one my favorite Zen sayings. (If I'm too literal about it, it makes brushing my teeth difficult.) It's just a cool, pithy way of saying that there is no un-special thing, no un-sacred place, no moment or person or thing or non-thing that's unworthy of respect, understanding, and kindness. To treasure, to revere takes a heart of devotion. Our vow is reverence, to revere what's here.

Devotion, repentance, training. It's interesting—and important—that Hakuin lists them in the order he does, with devotion first, the quality that he imagines gives rise to the other two. Devotion is "love, loyalty, and enthusiasm." When our hearts are aligned with love, what comes from us and our activity can't help but be loving.

Repentance is, in my understanding, to acknowledge truth as truth and be willing to change one's heart-mind about life. It might mean feeling guilty when we harm self or others, but it doesn't mean feeling ashamed. There's a world of difference between "I did a bad thing" and "I *am* a bad thing." One is helpful awareness and the other is not.

The last one—training—is pretty straightforward for us, as we understand meditation to be central to Zen practice. And yes, training refers to our spiritual practice in particular, but also our life in general.

And Hakuin says: Devotion has its source in zazen. Repentance has its source in zazen. Training has its source in zazen.

Which means, in essence, that devotion is awareness of, and compassionate presence to, your own experience. Repentance is awareness of, and compassionate presence to, your own experience. Training is awareness of, and compassionate presence to, your own experience.

Through the lens of this loving awareness, all is complete, nothing missing, nothing left out.

UNLOADING LOADED WORDS

Devotion. Repentance. Training. These can be loaded words.

If you're like me (and most everyone else), there are particular terms that just rub you the wrong way. Let me see if I can hit any of those trigger points. How about *obligation? Spiritual authority? Religion? Duty? Service? Submission? Holiness? Love, worship, faith?*

Words like *devotion, discipline, religion, worship, faith* need to be properly understood before we attach to them or throw them out. So let's talk about some loaded words for a few minutes. Words like *discipline, religion, love, worship, devotion, faith* point to and express essential spiritual concepts, and because of our cultural overlay, they are loaded with many layers of baggage, both personal and collective. As a result, many of us disregard them or actually meet them with aversion. This response makes a world of sense, but we are at risk of losing something precious if we are caught by own reactivity and anger.

Why do humans get angry? Usually we get angry because we've been hurt.

If I was taught as a child that getting beaten was "discipline," then I'm likely to hate the word *discipline*. I was hurt around the word *discipline*, and those old wounds are unhealed in me. So I can only see the word *discipline* through the lens of my hurt, my anger. I cannot see it clearly.

Once I recognize this, I have two choices:

1) Never use the word *discipline* or get angry when others use it. This is essentially insisting that my experience with the word *discipline* and my response to it is the "correct" one. This option is far and away the most popular, and it offers us no change, no understanding, no growth, no healing. It's the popular choice because we don't have to do anything different or difficult. It's just childish reactivity and we all already do a lot of that, so it's easy.

2) This is the harder choice: Do the actual healing work. Understand that I feel angry when I hear that word. Understand the hurt that's underneath it. Heal the suffering with compassion patiently, gently, thoroughly. Learn my trigger word's original or actual meaning (in this case, it's "to disciple" or "to learn"). Finally, make a new decision, through a clear and healed lens of perception, about whether or not that word has value for me, and use it—or not—accordingly.

Let's reexamine these words and maybe rediscover them. Let's look at what they are, what they actually mean, and then make a clear choice. (And *clear* means "with clarity and kindness.")

NOTICING OUR STATE OF CONSCIOUSNESS

So now, going back to the Song, we have another new vocab word: *paramitas*. *Paramita* means both *perfection* and *a raft with which to travel from the shore of suffering to the shore of liberation*. So, it describes something wonderful, a quality to aspire to and cultivate in ourselves.

There are six paramitas in Buddhism:

dana, generosity

ksanti, patience

sila, ethics, the discipline of refraining from harm

virya, diligence, persistence

dhyana, meditation

prajna, wisdom

The depth of each of these contains all the others, and each one could make for a lifetime of focus for practice. And these *all have their source in zazen.* Hakuin saw zazen—awareness practice—as the source or ground of all spiritual inquiry, practice, and everything he lived and taught.

Just like zazen, devotion, repentance, and training, the paramitas are not just practices (things to do) but ways of *being.* They're states of consciousness to simply rest in.

In 1890, psychologist William James wrote, "My experience is what I agree to attend to."

The place our attention rests greatly influences the experiences we have, and the experiences we have determine the life we live. So, making conscious choices about where our attention should go is a hugely important ability to possess. Putting your mind where you want it, when you want it there, for as long as you want it there, is like focusing diffuse sunlight with a magnifying glass.

If we can learn to discipline our minds, we learn to discipline our lives.

If you'd like to explore this, try choosing a way of being or state of consciousness that you aspire to as a daily focus for a week. For example, post a note that says "generosity" on your steering wheel, your kitchen cabinet, the corner of your computer monitor, and your desk at work. When you see it, you'll be reminded to reflect for a moment. Maybe something like, *Where is "giving" right now? What am I offering freely to others and the world right now? What am I receiving right now that was offered freely by others and the world?* This reflection might bring you to the awareness that by slowing your car down, you just offered another driver a larger space in which to merge. Or you sent someone a helpful link to a website you thought they may benefit from seeing. Or you accept the air around you as your breath with increasing ease and you realize that you're grateful for its simplicity and omnipresence.

CONTAGIOUS LIBERATION

It's not just Zen Buddhist zazen but awareness itself that liberates and transforms karmic suffering, breaks patterns of pain, and turns sadness into hope, thirst to overflowing, poverty to wealth, being lost to being found, darkness to light, ignorance to knowing, the prison of unconsciousness to the freedom of *awakeness*.

I hear that liberation and transformation in the *Oh* at the start of this stanza. *Oh* isn't a word, really, it's a sound we make to express something preverbal. We use *oh* to express surprise, appreciation, thoughtful consideration, awe, and wonder. It's a "wake up" sound. It's what we say when we just got a little bit bigger.

Awareness itself is contagious. And specific states of consciousness are contagious too, which is why you start feeling angrier after hanging out with your angry friends arguing about politics and why you feel more expanded and loving after hanging out with Thich Nhat Hanh, the Dalai Lama, Archbishop Tutu, Malala Yousafzai, Howard Thurman, or your own teacher. ("Hanging out with" can mean reading or watching too.)

Awakeness spreads and expands. Consciousness evolves itself. That's why Earth went from no life to simple life to complex life to human life, and why human life itself continues to evolve from entirely animal nature to simple reasoning, to complex reasoning and logic, to transpersonal and compassionate beholding, to unitive, enlightened awareness.

REVISIONIST ENLIGHTENMENT

I take only one issue with the Song, and the phrase *of the Mahayana* is it.

I have no patience for our infamous Zen smugness regarding

religion. What I'm talking about is the sometimes subtle, sometimes obvious, *I know better than my neighbors because I do Buddhism* thing. It's sad, but the truth is that I see this a lot.

I have to translate *of the Mahayana* here in my head to make it helpful. I translate it into "the biggest possible vehicle that includes everyone and everything throughout space and time."

The word *Mahayana* does mean "Great Vehicle," so perhaps I'm within my rights to do that. But I'm guessing that old Hakuin was making sure we knew that Mahayana practice was seen as separate from, and superior to, Theravada, Pure Land, Chinese Buddhism, or anything else.

This is what we humans do, isn't it? We really want our way to be the best way because we're scared that we're not good enough.

We like to imagine that Buddha and other spiritual teachers are enlightened beings, and that "enlightened beings" means "in keeping with our current twenty-first-century ideas and cultural sensibilities." We turn our pick-and-choose understanding of Dharma into a way to support our already-existent ego patterns and beliefs. We reimagine Buddha as a psychologist, or a feminist, or a civil rights activist, a super chill groovy spa dude, or a savior, depending on our current needs. We ignore the parts of scripture that don't seem to support our view or that we find offensive or shocking. They must not be part of the tradition. Buddha couldn't have been sexist, arbitrary, or ego-centered in how he taught his Dharma. Famously cranky Chinese Zen teachers couldn't have been ruthless or mean in their teaching and life; that all must've been deep teaching *disguised* as hitting and yelling. Famous Japanese Zen teachers couldn't have been racist, sexist, selfish, or the victims of unenlightened magical thinking.

The idea that our mythological teachers are aligned with us makes us feel secure and ever-so-slightly superior, doesn't it? So we are forever reinterpreting these ancient teachings so that they correspond with a worldview that we can understand and support.

This is universal; we all do it. We have heroes and we either align our lives to theirs or we align their lives to ours. Usually, a bit of both.

"Faith is a hammer with a book for a handle," singer and rapper Dessa says in her song "Ride," and she's right. We can use parts of ancient Buddhist scripture to get to, "I'm right, and the Buddha says so" if that's where we want to go.

This is how we unconsciously take something called "Dharma" (or the Gospel, the Vedas, the Upanishads, the Torah, the Talmud, the Koran, etc.), which is designed to tame our egos, and use our understanding of the teachings to support our egos instead. If we want to hang onto our racism, sexism, homophobia, or other pet hatred, it seems we can always find some scripture that supports that and ignore the other part that says, "Love your neighbor as yourself."

It's easy to see why we all do this. Can you feel the insecure kid underneath that? (What does that kid actually need—to be right? Or to feel secure in his place in the universe?)

But I've practiced over the years with far too many beautiful people who had deep, profound, and luminous practices that were not Mahayana Zen Buddhist zazen—to buy the idea that we're better.

And I don't believe "our" zazen is ours, nor do I believe that it's better. What would "better" even mean in this context, anyway? And how would we even measure it? If I'm sitting zazen next to my Dharma brother Ben, who was trained the exact same way in the exact same temple by the exact same teacher, are we doing the same zazen?

Comparison is always odious, and in this arena it's especially so. "Comparison is the thief of joy," Teddy Roosevelt said, and it seems to me that about 95 percent of the time, he's right.

So let's sing our highest praise to zazen and relax the Mahayana bit.

We can let Mahayana include everything—*everything*—and then stop worrying about who's in and who's out.

THE HOLIEST THING IS COMPLETELY ORDINARY

With all that said, I think it's also significant that the object of Zen's highest praise (at least according to Hakuin) isn't a thing or a person, it's an activity. And it's an activity that we can do, every day. This highest praise in Zen, the holy of holies, is literally an *everyday activity*.

Zen is an orthopraxy (practice-based faith) rather than an orthodoxy (belief-based faith). This is because, regardless of how lofty and beautiful our ideas and understandings may be, they usually do little to change our hearts unless they are married to experience. Ideas about water will not quench your thirst.

Ponder this: To sit zazen is to go beyond the doctrines of Zen, to go beyond Zen itself. "Go beyond Buddha," Dogen Zenji implores us, and to sit zazen is to do just that.

Zen does not regard life as a problem to be solved. We do sometimes call it "the Great Matter of Life and Death," which sounds imposing. It is. Anyone who has watched a loved one die, seen the curve of the earth from a plane window, or gazed long and deep into the night sky knows that this is a formless, wordless question.

"What happens every spring is just a hint of the thing," the Benedictines say.

That thing.

> *Life and death is a great matter.*
> *All things pass quickly away.*
> *Awaken! Awaken!*
> *Do not waste this precious life.*
>
> —*Dogen Zenji*

And it is indeed a formless, wordless question, so its answer has no form and no words. Or every form and every word. So the response to the questionless question that we choose in Zen is to awaken, as Dogen advises.

And zazen is awakening. Zazen is the posture, the attitude, the embodiment of awakening itself.

The great Chinese Zen master Te Shan said the same thing this way: "Realizing the mystery is nothing but breaking through to grasp an ordinary person's life." There's no split in his heart between the sacred and the secular, between the infinite, holy mystery and doing the dishes.

Everyday mind is Buddha. Every place the wind carries us is home.

"There is nothing equal to wearing clothes and eating food. Outside this, there are neither Buddhas nor Ancestors," says the *Zenrin Kushu* anthology of Rinzai Zen.

No matter our state of mind in this moment, our awareness practice can become simple: When comfortable, we practice appreciation and gratitude. We practice Big Mind, no knowing, no separation. When suffering, we practice acceptance and hold suffering with mindful compassion.

Our form is how we know consciousness. Our consciousness is how we know form. We eat and walk and argue and laugh and pray with our bodies. We sit zazen with our bodies. Our skin sits, our flesh sits, our bones sit, our marrow sits. Our ego sits, our soul sits, our spirit sits. Who can say which is most sitting? Which is most "us"?

We can't possibly help but sit with our entire lives—all our memories and hopes and past and future. We can't help but sit with our joy and our broken heart and our first breath and our last breath.

Can you offer your life as easily as every natural thing does?

Of course. Actually, you already do. You can't help it. Your life is itself already a complete offering.

6

THE PURE LAND

Those who try zazen even once
Wipe away beginningless crimes.
Where are all the dark paths then?
The Pure Land itself is near.

Trying zazen even once *wipes away beginningless crimes.*

This is a powerful, even irrational, assertion. But it's right at home in Zen literature. Zen isn't famously rational.

Which is good, because it's supposed to be an expression of Reality, and our perceived human reality contains both what we think is rational and what we think is irrational.

So when Hakuin says even one period of zazen wipes away beginningless crimes, is he being literal? Or is he being poetic and inspirational?

Yes. Both. He's waxing poetic, but he's also being literal and expressing what he sees as an actual phenomenon:

One moment of simple, mindful awareness is a complete shattering of the patterning of conditioned consciousness.

We can see, in even one moment of stillness, the nature of the activity of mind—that it is unbounded and free, and that although everything we think, feel, and do expresses it, nothing we think, feel, and do actually leaves a mark upon it. In this moment of simple awareness, no crimes.

So we really do wipe away beginningless crimes during zazen. We remember the dimension of our life that isn't bound by time or space, past or future. It includes all those things, but it isn't limited by them any more than the sky is limited by its clouds. We start fresh. And our fresh start includes taking responsibility for our past actions, while remembering that those actions do not define us.

Setting down the burden of identity, and all it entails, is one of the great gifts of zazen.

THE "CRIME" OF IGNORANCE

The word *crime* reminds me a lot of *sin*, perhaps because of the language of my Christian upbringing. Crime and sin are closely related, and from a societal perspective, they are both relative. What's a crime in one culture is not necessarily a crime in another. What's a sin in one religion may not be a sin in another. When we start asking ourselves what crime and sin really are, at their core, it's an important turning point. We begin to seek an inner authority, not an outer one. We have to look ourselves in the mirror every day, not the church, the government, the culture.

Ultimately, there is only one "crime": ignorance. We call it ignorance, or unawareness, misunderstanding, unconsciousness, a blind spot. Or we just call it, "Oops; I'm sorry. I didn't see. I didn't know." And in the moment of seeing and knowing, we immediately forgive our previous ignorance, as we understand clearly that we simply don't see what we don't see, we don't know what we don't know. It's actually very simple.

There's an analogy that's sometimes taught to illustrate this, about someone carrying tall, heavy bags of groceries and suddenly having someone running into them, the bags dropping, and the groceries scattering. Their first response is anger, and as they are scrambling to pick up their groceries, they yell, "Hey! Why don't you look where you're going?" before looking up to see that the person who's run into them is blind. Their anger evaporates instantly, knowing that the person was innocent and actually, literally, didn't see.

Even more obviously significant crimes (e.g., theft, assault, murder) can still be understood to actually stem from ignorance. Intentionally hurting others displays ignorance of the truth: the truth of the reality of karma, the reality of others' sovereign needs, the truth of our interconnectedness and our belonging to each other. In fact, I can only hurt others when I'm ignorant of those truths, consciously or unconsciously. Perhaps none of this makes us feel that the people who've hurt us are more "forgivable," and it certainly doesn't condone or excuse anyone's pain-causing behavior. But it does help explain them, understand how they came to be, and perhaps open the possibility in us of connecting to that person in at least some way.

The origin of the word *sin* literally means "to miss the mark." It was an archery term that meant to hit the target but miss the center. That way of looking at sin changes completely my relationship with it and with the teaching inside it.

In zazen, we keep aiming for the center. And when we notice that we're missing, we aim for the center again.

The very act of noticing the missing and aiming again at the center is to hit the center.

THE THREE POISONS

Those who try zazen even once wipe away beginningless crimes.

Where are all the dark paths then?

When do we actually commit a crime against ourselves and others?

When do we actually commit sin?

We can start by understanding that both of those terms imply that we've *caused suffering in others or ourselves.* That seems to be the universal metric, regardless of how the rules are framed.

In Buddhism, the three main categories of Things That Cause Suffering are greed, hate, and delusion. The dark paths. The Three

Poisons. And they are all dark paths and poisons that every human knows intimately.

Everyone knows how much they suffer when they are possessed by greed. Buddha called it "wanting something you do not have." That place is hot and tight and small. Even if we're aware that what we desire won't help, the experience of greed can remain. It's an ache that can feel infinite, a meaningless and unquenchable thirst for saltwater. It's horrible.

And the same can be said for its opposite, hate. Buddha called it aversion, or "having something we do not want." We all know how much it hurts us to actively hate someone or something. Its very existence seems to afflict us. It's like creation is broken because this person or thing even *is*.

Hatred burns like fire and we long to release it. But usually we can't make it stop just by wishing it so. It has a momentum that owns us and a gravity that keeps us bound. Hate is always foolish, yet we all do it.

Delusion is primary and is what gives rise to greed and hate. I like the translation of *delusion* as "to misunderstand." It's having incomplete or incorrect information, a bad map.

We get greedy because we misunderstand what's happening. We think that there's something or someone we lack, and that by possessing that thing or person, we'll be complete or feel better. And since we misunderstand what's happening, what we need, and what will help, we get greedy.

I like this because it means that when I'm greedy I'm not also broken, stupid, wrong, or bad. It simply means that right now, I misunderstand.

That's more workable, more fixable than "broken, stupid, bad, and wrong" and doesn't have the same implications of shame.

THE BUDDHA'S ANTIDOTES

In the Buddhist tradition, we say that it's the Three Poisons that give rise to that suffering. But we also have an important story—the myth of the Three Temptations of Buddha—to illustrate the possibility of relationship and transformation, and to illustrate the nature of the loving observer that's needed to do this work.

The myth of the Three Temptations of Buddha is about how consciousness works and what spiritual practice is like. It's about remembering who you really are and keeping your seat. When we hear mythological stories like this, we can use our imagination to let it touch us more deeply. The details in myths are not literal people, places, and things. They're representative of parts of our own lives and are talking to us about something universal to the human experience. So we can have some fun entering into stories like this using our imagination. Our imagination is much closer to truth than our thinking narrative is most of the time, anyway.

My paraphrasing of the Three Temptations goes something like this:

> In about 500 BC, in Northern India, at the end of his six-year spiritual quest, a man named Siddhartha sits down under a tree and vows not to rise again until he has realized freedom and complete awareness. Mara the Deceiver starts getting nervous that a Buddha is about to be born. (Mara is kind of like a Buddhist devil, at least for the purposes of this story.)
>
> So Mara tries his best to prevent this from happening. He tries to move Siddhartha off his seat with the three temptations of greed, fear, and shame. He figures that these are the three best antidotes to freedom and awakeness, so it's a pretty good plan.
>
> Siddhartha is first tempted by Mara's three beautiful daughters, but they failed to move him from his seat. Siddhartha simply says, "I see you, Mara."
>
> Okay, that doesn't work. Since he can't pull Siddhartha from his seat with greed or desire, Mara tries pushing him off it with fear. He sends a terrible

army with a rain of arrows. But when the falling arrows enter Siddhartha's field of awareness, they turn into flowers.

Okay, fear doesn't work either. Finally, Mara addresses him directly, "What gives you the right to think you can become a Buddha? Who do you think you are??"

In response, Siddhartha simply reaches down and gently touches the earth.

Mara demands of him, "I have an army of terrifying demons behind me, millions of them, all bearing me witness. Who bears you witness?"

And then the Entire Earth Herself, in a voice as vast as mountains of thunder, says, *"I bear you witness."*

Mara is defeated and withdraws. Siddhartha becomes the Buddha.

Myths about how spiritual beings came to be are pretty common, and the idea of passing tests is too. There are scads of "you have to pass the test" stories out there, and the Buddha story is no exception. Jesus is tempted three times too.

Greed (desire, grasping), fear (hate, aversion), and shame (delusion, misunderstanding) are said to be the causes of all suffering. These three temptations are not unique to Siddhartha in 500 BC These are familiar to all of us, here and now.

Although these are presented as "temptations to overcome," it's better to understand them as Dharma gates—entrances to insight and learning, doorways to wisdom and compassion. And these are the three central, most important classrooms we all have. So we might as well get comfy with them, as we spend lots of time in each.

It's important to recognize that these are all internal dynamics, all internal movements. Temptation doesn't come from outside, nor does insight. In this kind of work, there are no downloads. There are only uploads.

Let's look more closely at each of them. As we do, see which of them has the most energy, the most juice for you—the one you can most relate to in your life right now.

GREED

Siddhartha is first tempted by Mara's daughters, named Craving, Boredom, and Passion. The verse says:

> *They had come to glittering with beauty —*
> *Taṇhā, Arati, and Rāga —*
> *But the Teacher swept them away right there*
> *As the wind sweeps a piece of dandelion fluff.*

Before we jump in, a brief aside: It's a cultural artifact and symptom of its time that this myth's metaphor uses young females as its example of a corrupting force. That says something about how women were seen in that culture and time, and also about how sex was viewed in early Buddhism. Through twenty-first-century eyes, this seems quaint at best and stupid, offensive, and vulgar at worst. (*C'mon, Buddha. You're supposed to be enlightened. Pick up your game.*) That said, sex is a powerful and archetypal energy, and it can cause us tremendous suffering if we don't have a healthy relationship with it. ("I vow not to misuse sexuality, but to be caring and faithful in intimate relationships" is one of the ten precepts for a reason.)

The first two temptations are greed (desire, grasping, thirst, craving, etc.) and fear (hate, aversion, anger, avoidance, etc.). Both are normal, standard-issue human responses to pleasure and pain (or seen another way, a response to needs being met or needs not being met). So they come from being consciousness alive in form.

All life forms have the "pursue what works and avoid what doesn't" impulse; it's life sustaining. It's also externally focused, and our ability to control the external world is limited at best. So if our contentment is contingent on external things being a certain way, we're unstable, vigilant, and anxious.

At base, both greed (or desire) and fear (or aversion) are our healthy attempt to stay well and upright, but for most of us most of the time, it doesn't stop there. Our desire and aversion become an ego project designed to help us feel less fear and shame.

On a day-to-day basis, our greed or desire shows up as craving, boredom, and passion, as the verse says. These feelings are so commonplace as to be invisible to us most of the time, especially the more common, low-level versions.

The arising of craving, boredom, and passion also sounds like most periods of zazen. In fact, these desires can keep us from even getting to the *zafu* (cushion) in the first place. Wouldn't playing a video game or eating chocolate cake be more fun than zazen?

Greed or desire—the First Poison—is anything we lean toward to lose our balance.

THE POWER OF NOTICING

According to our story, when Siddhartha sees the desire for what it is, he defeats it by saying, "I see you, Mara."

That's all he has to do, and "craving, boredom, and passion are swept away like a piece of dandelion fluff."

Buddha overcomes his desire simply by noticing that it's there. He names it, and it goes.

Desire begins to lose its power over us when see into it, and when we see through it. When we see how we create it, we can understand how to dismantle it too.

I find this is my own practice and life too. When I'm having a particularly strong craving to drink, I find that saying, "I'm an alcoholic" aloud to myself is very helpful. Why? Because in saying this, I'm identified with the one observing—and feeling—the desire, but I'm not identified with the desire itself. And I'm expressing an understanding too, because I know why I'm craving, and I'm reminding myself of its okay-ness. Okay, so I'm craving a drink. Big deal. Alcoholics do that sometimes. Right.

So it's the exact same thing as, "I see you, Mara."

Reminding ourselves to be the understanding, compassionate observer is powerful. Name what's happening. It can ventilate your experience of suffering.

In the moment of seeing something ("Hey, look, a badger!"), we're self-identified as the seer, not as the seen ("I'm a badger!").

This means we're less identified with our affliction and more identified with the observer of our affliction. (I say "more" and "less" rather than "are" and "aren't" because we aren't just observers. We still *feel* the affliction, which is not the case in badger noticing.)

Observation touches a very basic level of our functioning as humans. We create the self/other separation very early in our individual development, and it's our deepest and most persistent sense of separation. When we observe something, there's always a sense of space built in between the observed and us. Developing an observer is one of the first things we do in meditation practice. Without that observing sense, we are identified with our suffering.

So Buddha's "I see you" is much more powerful that it might first appear. He makes clear what he is: *the understanding, stable, and compassionate observer in an inherently participatory universe.*

And I'll remind you here that Buddha is a state of mind, not a person. We can all do this.

TRACING DESIRES TO THEIR SOURCE

Charlotte Joko Beck, the American Zen teacher, has some advice for us when we notice we're gripped by desire: look for its source, for its cause. What are the causes and conditions that give rise to desire?

We only want something when we think we're lacking it. The buffet has no appeal if you feel full. And *feel* is the key. You can have enough but not *feel* like you have enough. (It's called "America.") (Okay, that was a cheap shot. It's called "humanity.") How many cars are enough? How many TVs are enough? How many relationships are enough?

Buddha taught that desire is infinite, and we really get to see how true that is in our culture. "Never enough" is our collective mantra and it's helping to rapidly destroy the world.

So let's do what Siddhartha did: let's keep our seats, stay upright, and look very closely at that desire. When it shows up, ask yourself, *Am I really lacking? Do I really need this to be whole or to survive? What is this desire really about? How do I feel? What do I actually need?*

This isn't entirely about teeth-gritting self-restraint and "not letting ourselves have what we really want" in the name of some pious, holy lifestyle. It's about knowing deeply who we actually are, what we actually need, and what actually helps. And what doesn't help.

Under that tree, Siddhartha was unmoved by his desire. He felt it, knew what it was about, and he held it kindly until it dissipated all by itself. He set a limit with behavior he knew wouldn't help. He kept his seat. We can all do this.

FEAR, HATE, AND OTHER AVERSIONS

So, back to Mara.

Since he couldn't pull Siddhartha from his seat with desire, he tries pushing him off it with the opposite: aversion. This is the Second Poison, which can show up as fear, or in intensified form, as hate. It's anything we lean away from, therein losing our balance.

Our myth says that Mara sends an army and a rain of arrows, but when the arrows enter Siddhartha's field of awareness, they turn into flowers. What an evocative image.

And what an implication we find in this myth: Those things we fear become blessings when they are accepted as valuable, understood properly, and worked with skillfully. When understood as a Dharma gate, fear is a treasure trove of insights.

And although it takes time and effort for most of us, our arrows can become flowers. Each of our fears tells us a huge amount about what we misunderstand, what happened to us, where we've been wounded, and where we're stuck. By definition, that's a gift.

But as with desire, many of our fears actually wither and die when exposed to the light of our insight, like a kid turning on the light in her room and seeing that the monster is her bathrobe flung over a chair.

When fear next arises in you—and it's better to do this with a smaller fear—talk to it. Say, "I see you, fear. You've come to tell me something. What is it?" It will tell you a story about being hurt. Listen to it with kindness. Inquire further. Ask questions. And above all, *feel* the fear, at least a little. The story around the fear is how it stays big, so don't feed that story. Just stay with the feeling itself with your kind, spacious awareness.

And look carefully at your desire to let it go. "Let it go" is a commonly misunderstood spiritual teaching. "Don't hang on" is supposed to be the spirit of it, which is lovely. But it's usually understood to be a nice, subtle variation on "get rid of what you don't like." In other words, aversion. Avoidance. Ignor-ance. In the short run, it might look good, and even feel good, to turn away from our suffering by "letting it go." But in the long run, that doesn't work. The seeds are still there.

What's better is to ask, "Why do I cling to something that hurts me?" That's not a dumb question, and the purpose isn't to send us into a nice shame spiral when we ask it, because we ask it without judgment.

Why do we cling? Because there's a benefit. Always. There's always a met need or a comfort or a habit or a reason. Look for it and you'll find it. That will help you have some understanding for yourself, some compassion for both your suffering and for the tactic that you use to try to not feel some of it. *Just see it.*

So practicing *let it be* is better than trying to *let it go. Let it be* turns into *let it go* all by itself.

The key to this part of the myth is that the arrows are transformed. They are recognized and accepted as arrows. *And they are not destroyed, but they are transformed by our awareness*—our choices, our compassion, our love.

When we look deeply into our fears and feel them with our kind attention, they can tell us their stories of pain and we can begin to heal them. Then fear isn't an enemy to kill or ignore, it's a friend who needs attention, a friend who wants to keep us safe.

Again: Fear is a signpost to freedom. Freedom is a choice we make. Be a commitment to that choice. Please practice as if your freedom depended on it. It does.

Arrows of fear really can transform into flowers.

It happens all the time.

SHAME'S STORY IS A BIG LIE

Okay, last one: shame. This is the one that has the most juice for me, because I see this one every day in my work as a Zen teacher and spiritual director.

We all get shame, regardless of the specifics of our religious, cultural, or family origin. How much we get and how that manifests varies greatly, of course, but shame is the great socializing force and is universal to the human experience. It's just a boring old fact: We're tribal beings and we're all hardwired to seek the approval of others. Shame is a great socializing force and humans need it to not only create culture but also to evolve and grow. Shame is not, in and of itself, a problem. It's when we don't see the shame we're motivated by and we let it run our lives that we're in trouble.

In our story, Mara *the Deceiver* is trying to get this Buddha-about-to-be to move off his seat because he knows that a Buddha is about to happen, and that's bad for the Mara business. And he's tried the usual—fear and greed—to move him, but no dice. So he pulls out the big guns on the third try, demanding, "Who do you think you are to be sitting there? What gives you the right?"

Shame, shame. The ultimate deception.

Note: This is not guilt (*I did a bad thing*), this is shame (*I am a bad thing*). One of those statements is true and helpful (we want a conscience), and one of them is not.

Siddhartha was supposed to inherit and rule his father's kingdom, so this voice of shame is about family connections, social obligations, duty, worldly power, all the "Thou Shalts," fame and fortune, blah, blah.

We all know this shaming voice. It's the one that wants to keep us small, to keep doubting ourselves, to not risk, to hide and cower, follow all the rules, fit in, and stay quiet. It says we're bad, not wanted, not loveable if we don't. It says we have no right because we don't matter. It says we're broken, even when we're not. This is the inner critic gone mad. Shame is irrational and unhelpful judgment. It's also untrue. It's also universal.

The truth is most of us live our entire lives with many versions of Mara's shame lie in our heads. Some of us are plagued by it more than others. When it's a normal amount, we don't even know it's there. When it's a lot, we call it depression—this voice is so strong that it can become an actual physiological disease. When people hear *"who do you think you are"* loud enough, long enough, they can even kill themselves.

SEEING SHAME CLEARLY

Shame is Mara's most powerful voice.

Via suicide, it directly kills almost a million Buddhas-to-be every year on this planet and it indirectly kills millions more.

It wounds billions of others, all the time, every day. Including me. Including you.

Most of us never think to question this shame voice because we think that (a) it's ours and (b) it's true.

That's terrifically sad because it's neither. It's not yours and it's not true:

(a) That shame voice that lives in your head isn't yours.

No child on this earth is born with "I'm not enough; I have no right" in their head. We learned it from people who were just scared and ashamed and didn't know otherwise. They used shame to socialize us, and although there's not a gift in the shame message, there is a gift in the socialization. The unhelpful message of shame is an example of delusion in Buddhism. It's the third poison. It's misunderstanding Reality.

(b) That shame voice in your head is not true. It's a lie.

If you want to see how it's a lie, try this:

Think of someone that you adore, someone dearly precious to you. Hold them in your mind, in your heart. Now imagine asking them to listen to the same shame script that you so often think you deserve.

Say to this person that you love, "You don't deserve to be happy. You're awful for being exactly who you are."

Ask this person that you love, "Who do you think you are to try something brave and new? What gives you the right to express yourself? Why do you think you get to feel joy?"

When you do this exercise, you'll feel the Mara shame voice as the petty lie it is. You'll feel it as the stupid, small-minded idea it is.

We can live our entire lives by a small, stupid script that we didn't even write, just because we don't know otherwise. The words of Hakuin, and our own heart-minds of awakening, implore us to know otherwise.

So how did the almost-Buddha pass this next-to-impossible test?

How did he enter this Dharma gate and turn shame into wisdom and compassion?

Siddhartha's answer to Mara's "Who do you think you are?" was to reach down and gently touch the earth. That's all he did. The word for this "earth witness gesture" is *Bhumi-sparsha*. It's a good answer: to just reach down and touch the whole earth with one soft, warm, little human hand.

Then Mara demands of Siddhartha, "Who bears you witness??"

And the Entire Earth Herself says, in a thunderously vast voice, *"I bear you witness."*

This part of the story always chokes me up. It's just beautiful to me. I think it's beautiful because my heart knows that it's true. We are all, all of us, witnessed, supported, and loved in ways we never know. That's not feel-good New Age nonsense. It's fact. Consciousness holds everything.

The Jewish Talmud says, "Every blade of grass has its own angel that bends over it and whispers, 'Grow, grow!'" There are bodhisattvas everywhere.

So Mara knows he's beaten and he scampers off 'til next time. Poor guy.

Why didn't shame work on Siddhartha?

Because his mind is in mindfulness (zazen) a state of nonjudgmental awareness. Nonegoic awareness.

No judge to appeal to, no ego to cause a reaction in. No greed, fear, shame.

This is your mind when you do zazen too—that's why this teaching is so important. We hurt others and ourselves when we act from greed, fear, and shame. We have the capacity to act wisely and compassionately when we see but don't act from them. That's why we sit zazen—to practice this kind of awareness. To practice Buddha, to embody and be Buddha.

INVESTIGATING OUR AVERSIONS

Years ago, there was a fellow Zen student practicing at our center. For whatever reason, I had a real aversion to him. I always perceived him as a goody-goody who was constantly trying to outdo everyone else to win approval.

And without even knowing it, I spent a lot of time reminding myself of how difficult he was, how wrong he was, and how right I was. He had no idea I felt this way, and without knowing it, I was really reinforcing my aversion, strengthening it, polishing it.

One day while we were leaving the center together, we were making polite small talk. Earlier, I had noticed his name on the bulletin board's many retreat rosters and I asked him why he had signed up for so many retreat days in the coming months. I already knew why, of course: because he was an irritating sycophant.

But with tenderness and sincerity he said, *"I just want to be like you."*

Bang.

I felt touched … then humbled … then ashamed of myself. How long had I perfected a version of him that was irredeemably awful? What had I known of his intention? Why had I constructed such a hurtful narrative about him?

In the coming days, I saw it. I had experienced him as irritating because I felt threatened by him—always the first one at the sittings, always doing everything right, always sitting up so straight. *Just like I always tried to do.* No wonder I was scared of him! Somewhere in my head was the idea, *If he's good too, then I'm less good.*

These stories are reminders that this phenomenon is always true: We dislike people to the extent that we don't understand them. Which means that as spiritual practitioners, we are beholden to (a) notice when we have aversion to someone, and then (b) investigate why. What about them do we not understand? Can we learn something about them that might help us?

Either way, we are finally and most beholden to (c) hold the suffering of our own aversion with compassion.

In my story of the Zen student, it was the revelation I had in response to his comment that woke me up. That was his great gift to me. But my revelation didn't need to be dependent on knowing that about him. I could have gotten there by noticing (a) *Wow, I really don't like that guy,* (b) saying, *I wonder why,* investigating my own experience, and realizing that I was simply scared that I wasn't good enough, and (c) holding that fear with kind awareness, and when I felt ready, replacing my lie ("I'm not good enough") with a truth ("My value is noncontingent. It's constant, eternal, and infinite").

That would have decreased my reactivity to him, because with healing, there is less fear activated. Simple, actually, but profound.

The practice of investigating our aversion is one of the most practical and immediately transformative practices I can think of. Do it. Make a list of five people in your life with whom you struggle, inwardly or outwardly. Look at that list with acceptance ... even affection. Why affection? Because that list is actually intimate, isn't it? Those names represent parts of you, and those parts of you are suffering. We come by our suffering honestly, and we come by our defenses against that suffering honestly, too. No, we don't want to live small lives that are defined by our defenses, fear, and anger. But we have to start by accepting that they are there, understanding how they came to be, appreciating how brilliant they are, and how they kept us safe ... or at least tried to. There's no enemy here. A list of people you're cranky at isn't a list of your personal failings. It's a list of symbols of your suffering and it shows you how you've been hurt in very real ways.

Once you can look at your list with some acceptance and warm understanding, ask yourself why your anger and aversion arise. These people are just the spark, but the gunpowder lives inside you already. What is it? What do these people each represent? What old suffering in your heart-mind do they activate? When you've found that suffering, hold it. If there's a lie there, tell it the truth. Be the force of benevolent awareness you so long for, so deeply need. Be it. Holding suffering with love is to heal the world directly. It's immensely powerful. It's participating in grace. So, in a way, this myth about Buddha isn't a myth; it's real. And it's not about Buddha; it's about all of us.

JUST KEEP YOUR SEAT

We deal with temptations all the time, both on and off the zafu. We are learning how to relate to craving, boredom, and passion. We are learning how to relate to fear and shame.

We do it in subtle and obvious ways:

- the poem we choose to share with someone
- the feeling we choose not to run from but listen to and feel
- the falsehood we recognize and correct

- the dream job we dare to apply for
- telling someone we like, "I like you"
- telling someone we love, "I love you"
- the hurtful thing we think but decide not to say
- the abusive relationship we decide to change or leave
- sitting zazen with dignity; enacting Buddha; becoming Buddha

This story of the Three Temptations exists to normalize our experience of practice both on the zafu and off it. This story is intended to be about us, to help us, because these temptations arise constantly. We're always tempted by the autopilot, by unconsciousness, by habitual ego functioning. So we always have ground for practice, and we always have a chance—in each moment—to make where we are the Immoveable Spot, not bound by greed, fear, shame. Mara wants to move us from our seat, and our job is to keep it.

The more we practice, the better we get at keeping our seats.

As you sit there where you are right now, are you not sitting on the whole earth?

Where else can you sit?

Ask yourself: what bears me witness?

When you hear Mara's voice, just say gently but firmly: "*I see you, Mara.*"

The ability to do this simple zazen practice and find our true, immovable seat belongs to each of us.

The right to reach down and touch the Entire Earth belongs to each and every one of us. Please do it when you need the support. Really! When you feel insecure and scared, remember *and feel, in real time*, the stability of creation underneath you with your own feet. When you feel stuck and frustrated, remember *and feel, in real time,* the dynamic and ceaseless flow of creation in the sounds you're hearing, the movements of cloth against your skin, the constant flow of your own breath, each different than the last.

Because just like she does for the Buddha, the Entire Earth Herself bears you witness in every moment, and she never argues for your smallness.

Instead, she is always bearing you witness, helping you to keep your seat.

Again, the Three Temptations, the four words ("I see you, Mara"), and the one gesture (earth-touching) are all describing internal movements.

So if enlightenment is acceptance of what is and compassion for suffering, then here we are. Always here, where what is *is* and where suffering can be found. No matter how far we get away from ourselves, we can always find our way back. Here's our temptation, here's our practice. Here's our seat.

7

ENDLESS
BLESSINGS

Those who hear this truth even once
And listen with a grateful heart,
Treasuring it, revering it,
Gain blessings without end.

People, being what we are, can't answer life's impossible questions without falling into the trap of illusion. Knowing this, Zen doesn't try too hard to answer speculative questions. These are not the central issues for Zen. What really matters is the here and now, because that's all there is. Zen accepts the idea that people are just people.

And, as humans, we get to ask metaphysical questions. We also get to realize our limitations and inability to answer those questions with any objectivity, because we cannot have any. We only know our minds. Life is like a dream, an illusion that we perceive through the filter of our personality, our experiences, our selves.

No one can arrive at and stay at the answers to the deep questions about life and death ... not for long, anyway, because of the constant changes in both perceiver and perceived. Blaise Pascal said, "It is a disease natural to man to believe he possesses the truth." So there's the rub: pursuing something is one thing. Believing yourself to finally possess it is quite another.

Nevertheless, we revere truth in Zen. We are disciples of truth. The image on the altar in the traditional zendo is Manjushri, the bodhisattva of wisdom. But truth isn't regarded as the Truth with a capital T. We don't mistake relative truth for Absolute Truth.

WHEN TRUTH IS NOT TRUE

As soon as we grab something as in any way absolute or "truth," we lose that which we seek. Truth flows like everything else. Truth doesn't land, or stick, or stay. Relative truth is like a housefly.

"A fly was very close to being called a 'land,' because that's what it does the other half of the time," said comedian Mitch Hedberg. We could say, "Relative truth was very close to being called a 'lie,' because that's what it does the other half of the time."

For example, it's true that donating money to that charity was a great thing to do last year when you had the money and trusted that they did good work. But it's also true that donating to them this year is not a great thing to do, as you don't have the money and have since learned that much of their donations never reached the people they were claiming to help. "Donating money to a charity is good" is a relative truth.

This is why it's said, "There are as many Bibles as people who read it." We can only see and understand spiritual teachings at our own level of awareness. No matter how advanced the teaching, it falls on deaf ears (or "pearls before swine," as Christ said) if we're not able to take it in.

Some of Buddhism's most advanced teachings on the nature of the self and the nature of karma have been misused for centuries to justify war and murder.

"There's no 'self,' so there's no murderer and no murdered."

"Yeah, I killed him, but I was simply advancing his karmic path."

"Since there's no birth and no death, there's no suffering or morality either, so I can do whatever I want."

Crapola, right? Those are all attempts at what's sometimes called "spiritual bypassing" (or spiritual materialism, ego hijacking, spiritualizing the ego, etc.). It's essentially when we're using spiritual or religious practice to support, sustain, benefit, or comfort our small, scared selves (our egos) instead of using it as it's intended: to help us see that the truth of who we are isn't bound by the ego's fear at all, but is actually consciousness—love—itself.

Spiritual bypass is also universally done, by all of us, at least to one degree or other. And it's almost always done unconsciously.

Some popular—and more extreme—examples might be using scripture to justify hatred or injustice, claiming hurtful behavior like sexual or physical abuse as "enlightened activity," or claiming to be above the law.

If our practice is one that's designed to keep us comfy and small, to reinforce our fixed beliefs about right and wrong, to help us avoid suffering and stay blissed out, then it's a good bet we're doing some spiritual bypass.

TRUTH RECOGNIZES TRUTH

Katagiri Roshi said, "The point of the spiritual life is to realize Truth. But you will never understand the spiritual life, or realize Truth, if you measure it by your own yardstick." It is truth that recognizes truth. That part of us that recognizes truth, treasures it and reveres it, is already a taste of truth itself. Ignorance doesn't recognize or appreciate truth—that's why it's ignorance. "Our own yardstick" (ego) isn't long enough for truth. But truth can recognize truth, and in that instant of recognition, we resonate with what we seek.

Zen uses the famous metaphor of Zen itself being a finger pointing to the moon. Don't mistake the finger for the moon. Zen is relative, the finger. The moon is absolute, and the finger never touches it.

But we still want the power of the pointing to pierce us. We do long for truth, love, awakeness.

Awakeness recognizes awakeness. Awakeness is contagious. Life creates life, awakeness creates awakeness. The Buddha was said to have left flowers in his footsteps as he walked.

The truth to which our friend Hakuin refers is "the Pure Land itself is near" and that something as simple and powerful as zazen is both the vehicle and the embodiment of enlightenment. The truth is that no one is left out, no one left behind. You don't need to rely on the good graces of the gods for deliverance, and no one gets into Nirvana on Buddha's back. The possibility of freedom and the power to transform—and even end—suffering is yours.

So what is truth? How do we recognize it?

Truth shows up as wisdom and compassion. That's Buddha.

Compassion is to be "with suffering." It's not a distancing action; it's a connecting action. It's *willingness to be with.* We emphasize the "with suffering" part so much because it's the part that needs to be emphasized. Being with contentment or happiness or comfort is not a problem for most folks; they don't need much help there. But being with what isn't easy to be with—that's where we need the help.

Imagine your best friend telling you that they love you so much and always want to be with you—but only when you're happy and fun. "I'd prefer not to hang out when you're sad or angry, but I totally love you."

We can feel the disconnect there. We can feel the edges of their "love." We know that love isn't actually like that. Love doesn't have preferences. "The Dharma makes no distinctions," my teacher told me once.

TRUTH DOESN'T LET US STAY SMALL

A life grounded in an unwillingness to be with the truth of suffering is a scared and small life. A spiritual practice based on avoiding what hurts is just an avoidance tactic. It's like a firefighter waiting for the fire to go out before going into the house. "I wanna be a fire fighter, I wanna look cool, but I don't wanna get hot or dirty."

For example, for the first few years of my sobriety, I needed regular AA meetings and regular contact with my sponsor to stay on track. I really worked that program, and I needed to. But for me—and I'm speaking for myself alone here—after a number of years I began to see that I was using the program and the self-definition of *alcoholic* to limit my life and stay small. I experienced fear and used recovery to try to avoid my fear. "I can't go that way; that street has too many bars," or "I can't travel because I'd miss my meeting." To distance myself from my self-doubt or sense of inadequacy, I'd also use my self-definition label as a point of pride, like, "That guy has no idea what he's talking about. He's only a hospital treatment program person, not a true AA person like I am."

This is similar to the time when I wounded my foot and needed crutches and then a cane for a period of weeks to help my foot recover. After a while, the nurse told me I could wean off the supports and walk freely again despite the pain. Although it was growth and progress, I found myself reluctant to experience the pain of a healing foot as well as go without the nice attention and sympathy the crutches and cane brought me.

To recognize truth even once, to "hear it," as Hakuin says, can change one's life completely. We usually think that it takes a big lightning strike to have a significant change of heart that actually alters our life and changes our trajectory. We tend to seek conversion experiences or super-high highs for this reason, and we'd love a huge spiritual experience to come, remove all our doubt, all our sadness, all our delusion, all our shame.

This is kind of "magic bullet" thinking, wanting one thing—one experience—to do the heavy lifting of practice, to propel us forward at such a speed that we never need long for energy or purpose or momentum again.

But the way this actually shows up in nearly everyone's life is, instead, as a series of small hearings, small thunder rumbles, small experiences that accumulate and accumulate. Altering one's course by even one degree makes a huge difference on a long journey.

"It is wisdom that seeks wisdom," Suzuki Roshi said. When I first read that sentence, I was totally confused by it, as I had thought the exact opposite: that a lack of wisdom drives us to seek wisdom. But when

I think of physical healthcare, of "health seeking health," I can get to it. I think of my dead-stubborn Irish-German great-grandfather who refused to go to a doctor despite any symptoms of illness he had. It's easy for me to see how unhealthy that is, easy for me to see that, had he chosen to seek healthcare, it would have been a healthy impulse and that it would have been his health that was seeking health.

ALWAYS A BEGINNER

Just like our hearts, we need to keep our minds fresh, pliable, responsive, and resilient. Without flexibility in our perspective, we can become fixed and hard and our lives can become brittle. If you don't see this, go talk to grandpa about the kids these days and you'll see what I mean. We create some pretty deep ruts in our heart-mind with repeated travel. We forget that heart-mind was once an open landscape, a vast pasture, filled to overflowing with possibilities. It's sad, but it's the human experience. We call this open landscape and vast pasture "beginner's mind" these days, quoting Suzuki Roshi:

In the beginner's mind, there are many possibilities.
In the expert's there are few.

That's a great example of how Zen talks about absolute truth and relative truth. We need to remember the original boundlessness of mind, the openness of the beginner. In that space, there is no right or wrong, no good or bad, no better or worse. No expectations, no judgments. And this isn't some weird, altered state of consciousness that only Zen people know about.

This is you, when you were three years old, playing with blocks or pots and pans. We call it "play."

Play has no specific starting point or stopping point. In fact, it has no point beyond itself. It's what Dogen Zenji might call "self-fulfilling activity." No goal, no metric with which to judge it. Ask a kid what the point of play is, how they know when they're done playing, and how well they did at their play today. Their expression will tell you all you need to know about that field of mind, that field you still have but have forgotten. That's the field Zen specializes in, which is why I think of Zen practice as play and not work.

All that said, Zen isn't anti-expert. If I need to have surgery, I want the expert, not someone who doesn't know which end of the scalpel is which.

But the danger in the expert's perspective is that they can often only see the one expert way, and "the one holding a hammer sees a world filled only with nails."

I like to think the *blessings without end* that Hakuin mentions are the infinite number of chances, of moments, in which to start practicing. (Like now.)

In fact, when we look closely, we can't find any other moment in which to practice. "Being in the moment" sounds like some special accomplishment but is literally impossible not to do. We can't *not* be in the moment. Our minds can imagine other times and places, but they can still only do that in the moment. Using this moment to imagine another moment is still using this moment. There is no other moment.

So in another sense, we only get one moment, one chance, to practice. But that one chance renews itself infinitely. So whether we think of infinite chances or one infinitely renewing chance, we still have good news.

And since we have infinite chances, then we are all beginners, as each sitting is the first. Sure, zazen gets easier insofar as the posture becomes more comfortable and the familiar patterning of our consciousness becomes easier to recognize. But each sitting is different, and each sitting asks for our full engagement, the entirety of our body and mind. If we leave anything out, or phone it in, we miss a precious chance.

So we really are all beginners.

We are all also beyond labels like *beginner* and *expert*. There's no such thing as a zazen expert (or, God forbid, "Zen Master"), because zazen is not a known quantity and cannot be mastered. Zazen—and mind itself—exists beyond all of our ideas about it, including ideas like time, experience, mastery, success, and failure.

We just return to Original Mind, and that cleans the slate completely.

This means that your zazen is Hakuin's zazen. It is your teacher's zazen; it is Buddha's zazen. It is your zazen.

And it's also not yours at all. Sukuki Roshi said, "Don't ever think that you sit zazen! Zazen sits zazen!" This expresses the correct attitude toward the practice. Give everything to it, but don't make it yours.

NONE OF YOUR BUSINESS

Of course we want to, and should, pay attention to what effects our spiritual practice is having on our lives and on the lives of those around us. But if we're not careful, practice can become acquisitive and we start to unconsciously view practice as a quarter that we're putting into the cosmic vending machine, expecting the candy bar we're sure will come. That's not personal practice anymore, it's just selfish. We're in it for ourselves alone, for what we imagine that we get. Then our metric for successful meditation is how calm and comfy we feel when it's over.

Katagiri Roshi said, "Your zazen is none of your business."

So don't worry too much about what you're taking with you when your sitting is over. Don't try to get anything. Just give everything to it.

Do not miss it, not for one breath. It is your life.

With sincere effort, zazen's mark cannot be missed. It's like trying to be yourself: you cannot fail. It is already done.

Your zazen is none of your business!

And I'd add that your love is none of your business.

Your life is none of your business.

Why? Because your life isn't yours, and it isn't about you.

The part of us that's always asking something from our experience, always trying to grasp something, is a part of us that we relinquish during zazen.

So when our teachers tell us that our zazen is useless, that it's good for nothing, they really mean it. We cannot see it or measure it by usual standards. Zazen exists beyond our ideas of it, so we can relax and just let enlightenment unfold. We don't have to make it happen or push the river.

So zazen really is none of our business. Zazen takes care of itself, so we don't need to. Isn't that a relief?

So explore this: Try not asking anything—*anything*—from your meditation practice for a week. Just do it and forget it. After a week, check in with yourself, What did you notice? Did your relationship with your meditation practice change while it was actually happening, knowing you weren't asking it for anything? Did your relationship with it change off the cushion when you thought of your practice? Anything you notice is fine. *The noticing itself is the practice.*

THE BLESSING OF GRATITUDE

Those who hear this truth even once
And listen with a grateful heart,
Treasuring it, revering it,
Gain blessings without end

At the end of this stanza of our song, we can't be certain if the blessings come from hearing an expression of truth or from having a grateful heart.

The power of the grateful heart is its receptivity and deep insight. Gratitude automatically includes an awareness of our interpenetration. We can feel how our lives are dependent upon others, and by extension, dependent upon all things.

Gratitude cuts off our sense of deserving or of entitlement. Gratitude is the opposite of taking for granted, so when we're grateful we get a chance to see the world afresh, with beginner's mind.

Its mindframe is not an avoidance of what is, nor is it a counterweight or escape. In other words, what we call gratitude isn't simply calling to mind things we possess to help distance us from the pain of not possessing something. ("I don't have food, but at least I have air" is limited in its usefulness in addressing my very real hunger.) Gratitude is instead a deep, found experience when the intimacy of each moment is fully allowed and loved.

Gratitude is a felt experience, not an idea. When our hearts open and we see through their open lens, we see clearly, and there's an emotional dimension to that seeing. We call it gratitude.

Being around someone with a grateful heart is powerful, and we can catch that gratitude and come alive. We never get tired of being around gratitude.

It can sound trite from overuse, but the natural arising of gratitude is a dead giveaway that you're doing something right in your practice. Grateful, humble, joyful, connected, content. Watch for these in your life as you practice. They are great barometers and great ways of preventing us from getting too distracted by ideas of attainment or enlightenment.

They are universal human qualities, not unique to Zen Buddhism. The qualities that you cultivate in your own spiritual practice or specific tradition should become universal and connect you to everyone and everything.

We practice Zen to become Zen and to go far past Zen. Then we can truly practice Zen.

8

"BEYOND BUDDHA" IS EASY

Much more, those who turn about
And bear witness to self-nature,
Self-nature that is no-nature,
Go far beyond mere doctrine.

Hakuin's phrase "bearing witness to self-nature" is one of the best ways to describe what we're actually trying to do in zazen practice. It is not always a particularly comfortable activity—and yet one of the most common reasons I hear for people to take up meditation is to "quiet the mind" or "calm and center."

However, if we are to truly behold self-nature, we must drop our preferences for comfort over discomfort and a "quiet" mind over a "busy" one. If we are indeed to bear witness to the truth of our nature, we must be willing to bear witness to the self-nature that's already here, already happening. We must set aside our agenda for the time being and get real.

In accordance with the core values of nonviolence, our witness-bearing must be both truthful and kind. To notice with the clarity of truth and kindness is enlightenment. And it's a process, always unfolding, as what's here to witness is infinite.

Often, we can almost watch suffering parts of ourselves be drawn toward our loving gaze like moths to a flame. If our beholding is indeed loving, our experience will come to it to see itself in a kind and truthful mirror, to see what it really looks like.

Our enlightenment is also an unfolding of what's already here, but until now unseen, unrecognized, like unfolding an origami bull, star, or frog into a wide-open sheet containing all possibilities, then refolded with loving intention as a crane, a boat, or a butterfly.

SPIRITUALIZING AVOIDANCE

And yet, the subtle avoidance of actual self-examination and self-compassion is so common as to be universal. In my work as a spiritual director, the thing I see more often than any other is people using their meditation (or zazen, centering prayer, contemplation, etc.) exclusively as calming or centering practice. This is lovely, of course, and there's nothing wrong with all the variations of practice. But on its own it offers no corrective agent for change. It merely treats the symptom, never the problem. It doesn't go deep enough.

At the end of our meditation, we feel a little better because we've successfully avoided irritation for a half-hour, and we feel pretty chill and pretty regulated. So we leave for work feeling okay, but that okay feeling only lasts a few minutes because of traffic, the lousy weather, and our stupid coworkers, and we don't know why. And now we're right back where we started before our lofty-sounding spiritual practice.

An example of using meditation for avoidance rather than growth is our typical approach to something as common as boredom. When boredom shows itself in zazen, we take that suffering as a sign we're doing it wrong and we do something else, or we strain harder to stay with our object of concentration in order to stop feeling bored.

So we've either just judged ourselves as bad for not being able to stay peaceful, or we've judged being bored as bad and decided it's unworthy of being felt, understood, or explored. And that judgment arose and was obeyed as fact in a second or two at most. We didn't even see it—never knew it happened—and we're "experienced meditators" and "spiritual people."

Wow. What did we just miss there?

We just missed something so simple as to be easily missed. We experienced something uncomfortable (boredom) and we wanted to avoid it, and we used our spiritual labels and/or narratives to justify and explain that avoidance. And those labels and narratives sounded good, and promised less pain, so we did what we did.

That boredom could've taught us something, could have showed us something about what's under the surface of our heart-minds, but we didn't give it the chance. Somehow, we believe our pain can't be helpful, it can only be a sign of failure. So we judge it, or we judge ourselves, and we push the pain away. *The goal of meditation is to never be bored*, we may as well have thought. *Or angry. Or sad. Or off-center. Or irritated, disappointed, grief-stricken, lonely, greedy, confused, or gassy.*

I see people time and again who've been sitting for decades and can't tell me how they feel right now. I see people who have twenty years of centering prayer under their belts who claim that their prayer practice is the best half-hour of the day—and whose marriages are falling apart; whose children won't talk to them; who are angry, selfish, and deeply unhappy the other twenty-three-and-a-half hours.

In my case, for a long time, my zazen was—at least in part—an attempt to escape my suffering—not to recognize, accept, feel and transform it. I used zazen as a bandage to cover my suffering, not to peel the bandage back and address the wound directly. In medical terms, it's accommodative or palliative treatment (no hope of cure) not corrective or therapeutic (change and heal the cause of the illness itself so symptoms no longer arise).

Now, to be clear, there are times when we need to bandage and not address the wound. There are times when it's wise and loving to choose comfort over fearless and searching inventory. And there are certainly times when leaving the room—especially in the midst of a heated argument—is the wisest and best thing we can do in that moment.

But the understanding here is that zazen and the spiritual path is ultimately never about avoiding our suffering but facing and addressing it squarely. And that applies to our collective suffering as well as to our own individual suffering. Because those two kinds of suffering are ultimately non-separate too.

SEEING BENEATH A BUSY MIND

There is no suffering in a busy mind; there's only a busy mind. Sometimes mind is busy, sometimes still. Sometimes the lake has lots of waves, sometimes it's calm. Sometimes the weather is loud, sometimes it's quiet. So what? We don't call a wavy lake "bad" and we don't think of a cloudy sky as a problem to solved. In fact, we may instead just sit and watch it, which is much closer to what zazen is supposed to be in the first place.

And if/when mind is *busy busy busy* to the point of genuine difficulty, we can be skillful enough to know that it's a symptom of a deeper unrest in our heart-mind. What's causing all those waves? What's the origin of the problem our brains are trying so hard to solve? Where is the starting point of the rumination?

Earthquakes deep down in the earth's crust cause huge waves hundreds of miles away many hours later. Here, on the beach of our experience, we understand that waves are happening. So the question is, what happened hours ago to cause these?

Cause and effect—karma—means that so much of what we actually feel and experience is memory. It means that the waves we experience breaking on our shores right now are the result of earthquakes that happened long ago. And we misunderstand because we think that our reactions right now are about what's happening right now. Saying, "stop bullying me" is almost never actually about the person standing in front of us.

The fear and shame underneath "stop bullying me" is the memory. The person standing there triggered an old feeling, an old sense impression and the unconscious, but very real, memory of feeling small, helpless, and victimized.

Watching mind waves (thoughts) is often watching the effect of a cause that already happened. It's time travel, in a sense, because what we're experiencing right now is already connected to something that happened a long time ago. We use the word *pain* to describe our present-moment experience of discomfort. But suffering—the resistance to pain, the struggle against it—has its origins in the past. So to investigate the origins of our suffering is always about going back in time.

In real time, it might look something like this:

Wow, lots of thoughts today.

Any patterns?

Most seem to be future-based, problem-solving.

Are they connected to any emotions?

Yep, I can feel the anxiety under the problem solving.

What am I scared of?

The dinner party on Friday.

Why?

I'd feel so ashamed if things went badly.

What does this feeling remind me of in my past? How old do I feel?

*Being in Cub Scouts when I was about ten. How
badly that event went, how much trouble I got in, how
ashamed I felt.*

Ah. I must be doing all this planning to try to avoid
that shame from happening again, to avoid feeling
that feeling.

Now that I know what's going on, I can stop trying
to stop those planning thoughts and simply sit with
the memory of that fear and shame. It's not happening
now. I'm safe.

But I remember a very real experience and I can
hold that pain with great understanding, care, and
patience.

See? The compassion we have now changes the past because what
we're present to is the felt experience of the past. Experientially, it's
still happening *now*.

Patting and rocking a crying baby can be done from a deep desire to
connect to and help transform suffering in another. It can also be done
from a place of *shut up shut up shut up shutupshutup*. Then the rocking
is an attempt to control someone in order to feel better ourselves. In
this case, *rocking the baby is actually an unwillingness or incapacity to be
with our own discomfort.*

This is why it's so important to know what's going on inside us,
what's really motivating our actions. Paying attention to why we do
things frees us from our attachments to doing them or not doing them.

So "to quiet the mind" is already to miss it. Instead of seeing a busy
mind, we see a problem. We've just made the assumption that we have
a problem. We've just decided to make it go away. We now have something to control, overcome, and conquer. We treat our own mind like
an enemy.

HONESTLY SEEING OURSELVES IS ZEN

What part of ourselves regards a busy mind as an enemy? Is it our spacious, accepting, imperturbable Buddha nature? Or is it our fearful and perpetually troubled little ego?

Ego, of course. Using spiritual practice to serve ego is the definition of spiritual bypass. Noticing that we've done this is crucial because *noticing we've done it is not doing it.*

And my point here isn't that any part of this is bad as such. My point is that if we don't see what honestly fuels our life and practice, it will continue to remain unchanged.

Let's go back to our earlier example: during meditation, our boredom arose. *Why?* What was it connected to? What was it showing us about our heart-mind? Emotions are holy messengers and we come by all of them honestly. I'm not saying that the narratives that accompany them are true, because they almost never are (e.g., *That guy's a jerk; I'll be alone forever; I can't stand this another minute*). But I'm saying that knowing *I'm angry, I'm lonely, I'm hurt and scared* is knowing something deeply true about our lives, and that truth is connected to every other true thing. There is no enemy here, not even in feeling afflictive feelings. *Feeling bad isn't failing. It's feeling.* And Zen practice—like every other real spiritual practice—starts with what actually is and accepts it, blesses it for what it is. Then we can investigate it with acceptance and love and follow the thread of suffering. We can heal.

Asking what self-nature is, is asking what self is. Investigating self is Zen. Seeing through—and past—self is Zen.

Those who turn about and bear witness to self-nature ... go far beyond mere doctrine. Buddha taught that he looked for, but could not find, a permanent, unchanging entity to call "self"—not like we usually think there is, anyway. What we think of as a permanent, abiding self is found to be impermanent, changing moment to moment.

Think of the river analogy: *You can't step in the same river twice.*

That's pretty good, but when we look deeper, we realize: You also can't step on the same road twice. Or hold the same teacup twice. The road and the teacup are changing too, just like the river. And the "you" that's stepping into, walking on, and holding them is changing, too. There is only interpenetrating, dynamic change. That's the "doctrine" of Zen, if you could call it that.

We sit zazen, studying the self. We notice what shows up, the contents of consciousness. The stories, the emotions, the sensations, the body. We see our identification with all of that phenomenon as "self." When we begin to quiet a bit, we notice some gaps between the sensations and our ownership of them. We notice the gap between breath and the idea, *This is my breath.*

Once we see how we create self, self becomes less compelling, less convincing as a narrative. It's like an experienced carpenter knowing so well how houses are constructed that it's easy to see "house" as just an assembly of separate things, and those separate things as assemblies of separate things, and on and on. A carpenter knows that a house is actually an assembly, and the idea "house" is a simplification, an idea that serves as helpful shorthand for reference. My teacher calls self a "useful fiction."

And of course, knowing a house as an assembly doesn't make it any less a livable place to be, no less friendly and helpful. But knowing a house as an assembly can help us be less attached to the idea of "house," appreciating it for what it is, and not imposing ideas of a separate, abiding self that constantly needs defense and protection.

Self-nature? No nature.

Bearing witness to self-nature reveals no nature, or non-self, or only-nature, or emptiness. Bearing witness to self-nature reveals that Big Mind expresses itself through our small selves. We see emptiness best when it shows up as form. Divinity keeps incarnating as humanity. Eternity is so in love with the temporary, fleeting, flawed forms of time that it just keeps manifesting itself as them, over and over.

Dogen Zenji's teaching on this is clear:

> To study the Way is to study the self
> To study the self is to forget the self
> To forget the self is to be intimate with the myriad things.

THANKFUL AWARENESS

When we notice that we've wandered or begun to daydream during meditation, we can experience or cultivate thankfulness for that precious moment of awareness: "Oh, I've wandered!" Instead of judging ourselves as having failed ("Dammit, I wandered off again!"), we can rejoice that we've returned. Which of those two do you think is conducive to the creation of suffering, and which to the alleviation of suffering? That's a pretty easy question.

If our attitude is truly kind, we can naturally experience thankfulness for all our moments of awareness. And as awareness precedes gratitude, gratitude practice *is* awareness practice.

If during zazen I notice, *Oh, I'm angry*, that's a moment of insight, of awareness. Although it was already there, I didn't notice my anger before. But now I do! A moment of noticing, a moment of expansion (my awareness now includes something more), a moment of light.

And with that awareness, I now have agency. I can choose what to do in relation to my anger, if anything is called for. What do I do here? How do I care for this feeling? What might love look like in this moment?

Now I'm relating with more of what's actually happening, beyond my judgments of good or bad, and past my preferences for pain over comfort.

Zazen reminds us of our realness, the truth of our being, the truth we are, simply by being. Thus, zazen is the most real thing we can ever do.

And you'll notice that I'm not saying "comfortable" or "easy" (let alone "blissful" or "transcendent") in this description of the experience of zazen. Although it may indeed be all those good things, that's not the spirit of zazen, and not the point. The point is to drop all our defenses against what already is and rest in that beholding. We may well experience meditation as a continual movement towards and tending to the suffering parts of ourselves, if that's what chooses to arise into our awareness.

QUIETING THE MIND IS NOT THE POINT

It's common to imagine that the path of awareness and self-transformation is one that leads us to become steadily calmer, happier, and more comfortable. Probably because, in the long run, it often does. But going from Big Block of Marble to Statue of David takes a long time, and that long time is mostly digging and chipping with hammers and chisels. It's always hard, messy, tiring, frustrating work.

The temptation to misuse spiritual teaching to comfort and uphold the ego is omnipresent, and no one does it perfectly. The point is to bear it in mind and catch it when we catch it.

This is also a place in our practice where a teacher (or teachers) and a healthy sangha are crucial. These relationships are often the canary in the coalmine for us and bring things to our awareness that otherwise might not be known. We all have blind spots, undeveloped parts, and unexplored areas in ourselves. And relationships are unpredictable, dynamic, and always involve a certain amount of friction that can show us where our rough spots are, where our growing edges are, and where our work lies. The not-free parts of us can show where we long to be free.

There are myriad things we humans use to escape from our pain, some obvious and crude, some far more subtle and sophisticated. Most of us "spiritual types" (a hilarious designation, as it's absurd to imagine an alternate category) like to imagine that we're above simple, pedestrian (and lower, frankly) escapes and dead ends like money, fame, and power. We might look down our noses at our shortsighted brother-in-law for his constant money grubbing or think ourselves above our active alcoholic coworker who is obviously looking for a bottle to fill a God-sized hole in her life.

As spiritual people, we think we've transcended the obvious traps of chasing the stock market, cycles of cosmetic surgeries, or several Ferraris in our driveways. We know those tactics won't work, and that those are houses built on sand, not stone.

And we're right, at least up to a point. It's true that sex, drugs, and rock 'n' roll won't free us from suffering any more than money, fame, or good looks will.

And yet we imagine that our being spiritual or our religious identity or practice will eventually serve us well as a Get-Out-of-Suffering-Free card. Our starting point, almost always unconscious, is some variation on *How do I hurt less?* That's not, in and of itself, a bad thing, and it's certainly a powerful motivator. What is important to see is that that's the exact same motivation as someone chasing money, fame, sex, or the next high. That same motivation means the same metric for success: *How far am I away from my pain? How much do I hurt?* We unconsciously seek lofty stuff like wisdom and enlightenment because we think it will mean our hurting less, or not at all.

Again, it's important not to judge this motivation, but to see it for what it is, and to understand how it will shape everything that shows up on our path.

If we were radically honest, we'd say what we really think: *Spiritual practice is supposed to make us more spiritual and less human. We're here to transcend our humanity, our base natures, and not be ruled by them.*

And we'd be right, technically, but we'd misunderstand everything we'd just said, and we'd spend our lives practicing with a deep split in our psyches that would drive us father and farther from the truth, healing nothing and accomplishing nothing.

"To quiet the mind" is a perfectly fine motivation for wanting to take up Zen meditation, and it's the one I hear the most often. But where we go wrong is by addressing only the symptom (lots of racing thoughts) through calming, focusing, centering techniques and ignoring the cause of those racing thoughts. After our zazen is over, they come right back. It's like turning off the news broadcast that we don't want to hear about. We don't hear about it, but it changes nothing about what's really happening out there.

RETURNING TO OURSELVES

It seems to me that choosing to return to, explore, and feel the truths that we hold in our felt sense of memory in our body and emotions is like a salmon choosing to swim back upstream to find its original home, its spawning grounds.

We seem to have a sacred impulse to return to the space of our own making in order to reconcile ourselves to something dangerously real.

We seem to have an invisible intuition that demands that we reconcile our own opposites, that we shine our falsehoods with the light of our truths, that we become large enough to contain all our contradictions and divisions with the wide arms of wisdom's understanding, love's forgiveness, and compassion's reconciliation.

This upstream journey is arduous, and everything can seem to be fighting against that sacred homing impulse. Yet we persevere, understanding that to find the truth of our origins is to find the truth of our now, just as to find the truth of our now is to find the truth of our origins.

In zazen we can see the golden thread of truth that runs through all our days, regardless of how distant we may feel from it. We are drawn by the irresistible force of ourselves, the truth of our being, the love that we have always been.

"BUT THERE IS NO 'SELF'!"

Of course, I've already said that Buddhism offers the hypothesis that there is no "self" or "soul."

Soul is a loaded word in Western culture and has theological implications that may or may not have been intended. Personally, I'm not thrown by the word *soul*, or by the idea that I might or might not have one. I'm honestly not that interested. I want to do the very best I can, right here, right now.

Exactly what is happening, I don't need to know. In fact, I can't.

What happens next, I don't need to know. In fact, I can't.

What I can do is arrive fully in this moment and offer myself to it. Right here. This body, this breath.

This very body, the Buddha, Hakuin will soon tell us.

The first wave of Japanese Zen teachers offered their students no books to read and little explanation of the tradition beyond *just sit*.

In 1962, when asked if he should read any books about Zen to help begin his practice, a puzzled Suzuki Roshi responded by asking my teacher Tim in return, "Why would you read a book?"

This isn't a glib answer, nor is it intended to be a deep, inscrutable Zen response. Suzuki Roshi was genuinely puzzled.

This makes sense to me. When I was young, my parents made sure I was registered for Red Cross swimming lessons every summer for ten years. From Tiny Tots through Lifesaving, I spent summer after summer learning new strokes, new ways of breathing, treading water, and eventually helping carry struggling people ashore. In those hundreds of hours of swimming lessons, we read a total of zero books.

"I'm here to learn how to swim. What books should I read?"

"Why would you read a book?"

We mustn't mistake this for anti-intellectualism. Again, Zen, like other great contemplative traditions, is not anti-intellectual. It simply acknowledges that there are other ways of knowing than our usual way of memorizing, discursive thinking, problem solving, and conceptual overlays.

(Actually, why *are* you reading a book? Maybe you should put it down and go sit zazen.)

But people ask me about the "no self/no soul" thing all the time. It's very important to them. If it's important to you, too, take a few minutes to see if you can think of why that might be.

"I'm a Buddhist and Buddha said that I have no self, so that's that." I see this a lot too. People get excited about a new idea and a new belief system, and they imagine that they're part of an exclusive club that is privy to The Truth and they pity the poor idiots who aren't as wise or enlightened as they are.

Oh, goody. Now you can go argue with your Muslim, Jewish, and Christian friends who say that there is a self. Maybe you'll win the argument and get to be right! Think of how smug and self-righteous you can feel!

Then, if you're very lucky, your Zen teacher will pinch you and you'll say, "Ow!" Then she'll say, "If there's no self, smarty-pants, then who just said, 'Ow'?"

In my experience, saying stuff like "there's no self-nature" is helpful about 1 percent of the time. The other 99 percent of the time, it's a cheap trick, an escape, an attempt to sound cool. Suffering is real, even if the "self" that suffers ultimately isn't. So skipping to "no self" is usually a way of distancing ourselves from that suffering.

Same with the ideas we carry around about enlightenment: useful about 1 percent of the time. For the other 99 percent, it's useless, or worse, because we have no idea what we're talking about and our ideas of enlightenment are just daydreams of some perfect state we don't have or some imaginary Camelot that other people live in but we don't. (Worse yet is imagining that we ourselves do, in fact, live there, and we're "enlightened." It's not an accident that people we regard as seriously woke rarely if ever regard themselves as such. Almost without exception, "I'm enlightened" is a dead giveaway.)

The poor, perpetually insecure ego is constantly looking for inroads to feeling pride and is very skilled at co-opting our practice for its own ends. This is important to know and look for, because it will come up. For all of us. No exceptions.

When Hakuin says we *go far beyond mere doctrine*, he's reminding us, like every Buddhist teacher before or since, not to land on and cling to beliefs that suppress or pretend to answer the formless, wordless questions. Because that's actually not addressing the great matter of your life and death, it's ignoring it. That's killing it. Don't deconstruct and analyze your life's questions in order to have some tentative, illusory "answer" that will help you sleep better tonight but will stop working soon. That's using the wrong tool.

THE BYPASS TO NOWHERE

The Great Insight (the Buddhist doctrine of *anatta* or "no abiding self-nature") isn't the goal, nor—and this is very important—can we skip to that realization and claim it as ours. That's spiritual bypassing, and it causes suffering.

"Bearing witness to self-nature" is *recognizing suffering, then choosing to move toward it.* It's the opposite of spiritual bypass. And it's a continuous practice, not a destination to arrive at.

Spiritual bypass might be being "nice" instead of being authentic.

Spiritual bypass might be calling attachment "love."

Spiritual bypass might be explaining staying in the abusive marriage as "obeying God's will" or "exercising patience."

Spiritual bypass might be remaining silent in the face of injustice and calling our fear "self-restraint" or "tolerance" or "endurance."

Spiritual bypass might be calling shame "humility" and self-hate "modesty."

Spiritual bypass is the ego using the path for its own ends, instead of the other way around. It's forcing the truth of our heart-minds (or souls, if you prefer) to submit to the fear and shame of the ego, instead of the other way around. It's any and all forms of religious fundamentalism. It's giving away our self-responsibility (e.g., "Our scripture says so, so it's true and I don't have to worry about it anymore.")

In case you can't tell, there's a lot of it around, and there always has been. Our job is simply to see it when we do it. See it for what it is, accept that it's in us too, and then investigate what it is that we're trying to avoid. That's where the pain is, so that's where the work is. That's where we can heal.

JUST RELAX AND PAY ATTENTION

Explore your avoidance of pain in meditation (and life) and notice your usual stance of avoiding. *Just notice it.* Watch how your attention leans away from the traffic jam, the screaming child, the difficult co-worker, the song you don't like. *Just notice* the leaning away, and how it shows up in your thoughts, your emotions, and your behavior.

Catch yourself doing it after you've done it, then catch yourself doing it as you're doing it. Then catch it just before you do it. Then make a choice. Offering yourself a simple and profound invitation to hold the pain. Instead of leaning away, ignoring, distancing, explaining, justifying, rationalizing, analyzing, conceptualizing, just feel it. Literally, just feel the pain of that moment. Allow it. Hold it with acceptance, curiosity, kindness.

Now you're not scheming against it. Now you're not asking anything of it (to be rational, to be justifiable, to be normal, to make sense, to have "meaning," to go away soon, etc.). Now you're just with it, holding it with great care.

This is not soft or weak or saccharine. This is very hard work, too hard frankly for most of us to do for more than a couple of minutes at a stretch. This experience is not an idea. It is called *compassion,* and it actually heals and connects us, to ourselves, and to the world.

Who bears witness to your life? Can it be anyone's eyes but yours?

Who sees out of your eyes? Are you just the witness? Or are you the witnessing itself? Is there a difference?

And here's where it stops being trippy and abstract: Because your witnessing is the only witnessing, the pain you see and hold is the only pain. And the compassion in your witnessing is the only compassion that there is.

Your pain is The Pain. Your compassion is The Compassion.

Intellectual grasping of this is of little use. But moment-by-moment practice of The Compassion is of universal import.

It is not other than the entirety of the Buddha way itself, beyond ideas of Buddhism.

Go far beyond mere doctrine. Go beyond Buddha.

Don't dissect your life's questions, dance with them. Dance until you disappear, and only dancing remains.

9

DO THE MATH

Here effect and cause are the same,
The Way is neither two nor three.

A Zen teacher named Engo wrote, "When even one particle stirs, the whole universe is involved. When a blossom opens, the world responds. But what do you see when no particle stirs and a blossom does not open?"

A FLOWER IS THE UNIVERSE

Engo's words sound to me like an expression of samadhi, or "one-pointedness." It's a place of nondual awareness, where we experience our not-separateness from all things, the non-separateness of Reality itself.

This awareness collapses space as well as time. It collapses linearity, and therefore our usual understanding of cause and effect.

We are told that the entire universe responds to an opening blossom. The scope of that response is infinite, unbounded, timeless, limitless. It is more than the air around that opening blossom or the bumblebees near it that respond to it. It is more than the passing breeze borrowing some of its fragrance, or the appreciation in the eye of the passing person. The whole world, the whole universe, all Reality, known and unknown, past, present, and future, responds to an opening blossom. There is nothing that does *not* respond to an opening blossom. It all vibrates.

All you have to do to prove this teaching wrong is stop vibrating.

Everything is interconnected; all phenomena suffuse each other. Therefore, as Chinese Zen master Hongzhi says, "We are told that not a single thing exists." A "single thing" is impossible. It can't exist.

We have an impossible time trying to conceptualize the scale of interdependent, co-arising phenomena, or Reality itself. We just can't get it to stick in our heads. So we have a hard time with this teaching. Our limited experience doesn't seem to show that the entire universe responds to an opening blossom. In fact, it seems to tell us the opposite: that most flowers bloom unwitnessed and unappreciated—if they bloom at all.

To illustrate to yourself that a single flower doesn't exist, close your eyes and imagine the opening blossom that Engo talks about. Picture the flower in your mind, as clearly and in as much detail as you can.

Now, what non-flower things did your flower image include? Did it include the earth your flower was growing out of? The sky, the air that surrounded it? A stem and leaves? Other flowers, grass, trees in the background? Did your flower have roots? A vase? Water in the vase? Was it sitting on a table or altar?

Less tangibly, we know that the blossom included the seed it grew from, the soil, the rain, the sun, gravity, wind, the oxygen and carbon dioxide, the shade and the insects and the seasons upon the turning Earth.

Now do this same exercise using a physical object you've most recently purchased. Ask yourself what the creation of, and your acquisition of, that object depends upon. For example, if you recently purchased a nice nitro cold brew coffee from a coffee shop, you could list things like this: *coffee beans, sunlight, water, farmers, a Third-World labor force, ships or trucks, fossil fuels, plastic, petrochemicals, metal, infrastructure, real estate, currency, banks, refrigeration, fresh water, retail workers.*

EVERY THING IS KARMA

Years ago, when he was teaching about karma, my teacher Tim said, "Everything is both the cause and the effect of everything else." So pervasive and so complete is the interpenetration of all phenomena that separating things into "cause" and "effect" gets blurry.

Buddha taught that karma is *not* the universe's built-in justice system for rewarding good people and punishing bad people. It's actually just cause and effect. (We humans are the ones who add the morality layer to those causes and effects.) But with our interconnectedness being so profound and reality being so dynamic, those causes and effects are infinite.

Cause and effect means that we reap what we sow.

We *all* reap what we *all* sow. And actions, speech, etc., that stem from greed, hate, and delusion beget greed, hate, and delusion.

> *All my ancient, twisted karma*
> *From beginningless greed, hate, and delusion*
> *Born of body, speech, and mind*
> *I now fully avow.*

This is a verse called the Formless Repentance (or the Acknowledgment of Karma), and it's one of the verses in the Zen liturgy. In fact, after the robe chant that we recite before putting on our robes, it's the first chant in the service. We start here.

We call this the "formless" repentance because we're not listing specifics—we're making generalizations about our universal human tendencies. And before you freak out, "repent" actually means "to change one's heart in response to."

It's from the Greek word *metanoia*—"to change heart and mind."

To intend to change the heart-mind is what a vow is.

So the acknowledgment of karma is about starting with a clean slate. We find freedom in this acknowledgment, because it's true. And truth frees us.

Your karma is *ancient* and *twisted*. It started *waaaaay* before you, came along, so don't get too freaked out. Your karma includes your race, gender, nationality, biology. It includes your parents and your parents' parents and your parents' parents' parents. It includes hydrogen from the beginning of the universe. It's *beginningless*. You can't find where it started.

And *twisted* means it's very complex. Don't try too hard to figure it all out.

Thinking we know what action causes what effect is dangerous at best—it can easily devolve into control tactics ("Giving my partner flowers made them stop being mad at me") or an imposed justice system based on our limited understanding ("I got fired today because I tried to get my ex fired from her job last year"); it can even lead to magical thinking ("I wore my jersey, so my team won the game").

Despite my saying all this, I'm willing to bet there's a part of yourself that still thinks karma can be figured out, even if just in relation to yourself. Like I said, that can be dangerous—so to tame that overconfident inner skeptic, dare it to try. Find your karma. Spend some time with a huge piece of paper and write your name in a little circle in the center. Then, all around you, write the name of anyone and everyone you can think of who has influenced your life—for what you think is better and what you think is worse. Everyone. Start with the obvious ones: Mom and Dad, their parents, their parents' parents ... their friends, spouses, exes, kids, coworkers, neighbors ... all their parents, parents' parents, friends, spouses, exes, kids, coworkers, neighbors who influenced them who then influenced you ... all the people you've never met but who touched your life from a distance, like the people who made your furniture, clothing, electronics, and home ... the people who wrote the books and magazines and news stories you've read ... the people who painted the paintings and wrote the songs and founded the schools and delivered the mail and built the cars you've driven or passed or been passed by ... and all those people's parents, parents' parents, friends, spouses, exes, kids, co-workers, neighbors who influenced them. Then add all the names of the people that your life has influenced, in both small ways and in large.

The web of connection is infinite.

ACKNOWLEDGE AND ACCEPT YOUR KARMA . . .

We have to start by acknowledging that we're part of that infinite web. We own our actions, our karma, completely. We take responsibility for our response to it all, whether we think we "created" it or not. It's on our plate, so we eat it.

That's what "avow" means: to admit, to see, to acknowledge, to take ownership of.

We are interconnected beings. Our unconsciousness causes us suffering personally but it also hurts others. We hurt each other and ourselves all the time.

This is *not* an original sin thing about labeling ourselves as inherently flawed or broken or wrong. It's about acknowledging the universal human condition of suffering caused by our frequent misunderstanding of reality. We're not bad, we're just ignorant and confused—that's all.

Once we've deeply acknowledged the real impacts and interconnectedness of our actions, we can also acknowledge the fiction of karma: since everything is made of everything else, everything is infinitely reducible and non-separate, so everything is both the cause and the effect of everything else. It's not that there is no responsibility for what we've done, for who we are. It's the opposite: *total* responsibility. Seeing who we've been and who we are with complete clarity.

We are the sum total of all the decisions we've ever made, the collected karma of all our thoughts, deeds, and actions. We own them all, see them all. And when we see deeply enough, we see that they do not define us.

It's like clothes. When people see us, they take in our clothes as part of that picture. That's part of how we see ourselves and part of how others see us. We make choices. We can own that.

But our clothes aren't who we are. We can change them anytime we want, start fresh. These are our choices. See?

Taking responsibility for our past, taking inventory, making amends, is already doing something fresh and innocent and new. It's changing karma.

. . . BUT DON'T GET ATTACHED TO IT

Like many others in my tradition, I chant the Verse Before Shaving every few days before I shave my head and symbolically renew my vow to relinquish attachments and live for the benefit of all beings:

> *The bonds of attachment are hard to release*
> *Within our past, present, and future actions.*
> *Realizing the realm beyond karma*
> *Is the offering of true compassion.*

I first heard this verse when my head was being shaved for the first time, years ago, on the afternoon of my ordination ceremony. Three of us were being shaved, and several people were helping—cutting, shaving, and chanting throughout.

It was surprisingly evocative for me, although my hair was already pretty short at the time.

I realized that the person shaving my head—my friend Wanda— was the first person to touch my bare head in forty years, since I was a newborn. The intimacy of that gentle touch was shocking to me. Realizing that I actually had all of my hair taken away was shocking to me too. I surprised myself further by crying—at the beauty of the tradition, at the intimacy of the ceremony, at the strange and intimate sacrifice I was making for my spiritual practice.

Perhaps most surprising of all has been my ongoing decision to continue shaving my head, twice a week. My teacher doesn't require this of his students, so it's my choice to continue. The promise I made to myself was to continue doing it as long as it continues to teach me. Once it's taught me what it can, I'll quit.

I'll keep you posted on that.

> *The bonds of attachment are hard to release*
> *Within our past, present, and future actions.*

Yeah, no kidding! Those bonds are part of what we think of as "us," so we grab them tightly. Interesting, no? We tend to define ourselves largely by our current preferences and current limitations—not by our possible freedoms. These definitions become attachments that are limiting for us.

We cling to our past as part of our "self," as if pieces of our past were still defining and limiting us. ("I went to Harvard for my under-grad." "I spent a decade in prison." "I've been married three times." "I was born in Afghanistan.")

We cling to our ideas of future (our plans, dreams, and hopes) as part of "self," as if they were currently defining and limiting us. ("I'm graduating in two years." "I want to retire at 60." "I'm staring my own business first, then we'll have kids.")

And we cling to the present as "self," too. ("I work for UNICEF." "I own a Subaru." "I'm twenty-three years old." "I'm reading a weird book about Zen.")

This is one part of karma, the idea of carrying our past, present, and future with us and being conditioned by them by unconsciously letting them be our lens and limiting our worldview.

But we need to also acknowledge that our conditioning is real, and that small mind/small self/ego is a very real result of nature/nurture/karma too.

During zazen, we intentionally relinquish attachment to and iden-tification with arising phenomena. That is to say, we relinquish own-ership of thoughts, sensations, emotions, impulses, etc. We notice what's here and what's happening, but we don't feel compelled to label it, analyze it, separate from it, or own it. In other words, we're just *here* with *this*. In fact, we're not with it, we are it. We are here and this. No separation. Which also means no past and no future. No time. No beginnings. No endings. We realize *the realm beyond karma*.

The interesting bit is that realizing this *is the offering of true compassion*.

Why do we practice? Out of compassion, for the benefit of all beings. That's the ancient vow. Practice itself is the most fundamental level of compassion.

How do we offer compassion to this suffering world?

Realize the realm beyond our personal stuff, beyond our karma.

Why do we need to practice, to keep trying, to continue?

Because the bonds of attachment are hard to release.

It's taken me years to know this, because it's taken me over a thousand head shavings and recitations of this verse to figure out what it was trying to tell me. To figure out why it's traditional to chant something before we shave.

Your practice, your vow, your life supports me, just as it is. You support me and remind me of the vow just with your simple presence here on earth, just your willingness to practice and to try to learn a kind way of being in the world. I am grateful to you.

There's something powerfully transformative about shaking a stranger's hand and honoring the divine in them, sitting in silence and letting all barriers dissolve. This is the root meaning of conspiring. It's from the Latin *conspirere*, "to breathe together."

To sit with others is to live in the world. To live in the world is to be thoroughly vulnerable at all moments.

The realm beyond karma is here.

The offering of true compassion is you.

So, as always, the answer is inside us. There is no answer "out there" because there is no "out there."

There is only this, the undivided One. To go in is to go out, to go down is to go up. Let's aspire together, maybe even vow together, to keep going inside, finding the memories of suffering stored there, and meet them with an open heart of compassion.

FIND YOURSELF IN A TEACUP

Here effect and cause are the same,
The Way is neither two nor three.

There is an old koan about a Zen teacher:

Whenever he was asked about Buddhism,
Master Gutei simply raised a finger.

Master Gutei sounds like a character, and if this story is literal fact, probably pretty tough to work with. But it also sounds like he understood *neither two nor three.*

If I grow old and cranky and eccentric, I think I want to be a teacup Zen teacher. Whenever anyone asks me anything about Zen, I'll raise my teacup. I always seem to have one around, so it would be convenient for me.

I know you're rolling your eyes at me, but I think it would actually be very instructive. Because when you see the raised teacup—when you really see it—you see everything. Your whole life, the lineage of ancestors, your face before your grandparents, Buddha, Moses, Krishna, a stranger, a small plane taking off from a rural airport, the kindest person you ever met, a child's balloon, a moss-covered gravestone, the open summer field filled to bursting with sunflowers.

A raised pointer finger.

A raised teacup.

It's all here.

If you look past the teacup, you look past your life.

So I will take a moment to affirm that, yes, nondual, unitive experience is real experience. Flowers do contain the entire universe, as do we. Ordinary, non-magical flowers and tea and people and puppets and Wisconsin and your eyeballs are made of the entire universe, all the suns and stars.

But the important part is to know, to *feel* that this is true. Hearing this from someone else, even believing it, is of little use. But your knowing is of vital importance.

Why is your knowing so important? Because your conscious participation in the Buddha way is itself the vital functioning of the Buddha way. It is not other than the entirety of the Buddha way itself. Your knowing is important because your conscious participation in life is itself the vital functioning of life. No one can take away your knowing, and it is the only knowing that there is.

Do this: Go buy a teacup. Buy the plainest one you can find at a Goodwill store, a used one, an old one, a chipped one. Now, the next part of this exercise is going to startle you—and make a mess—so you may want do it outside. Or put down some newspaper.

Take your cup. Fill it with the tea you like best and hold it up. And hold it up and hold it up and don't stop holding it up until you can't anymore and then when you can't hold it up anymore, don't.

Let it crash to the floor, shatter, tea going everywhere.

Seriously. Let it shatter.

You'll see your reflection there in the spilled tea.

The teacup's life and death, your life and death.

You are neither two nor three.

Can you find your reflection in your life and death?

Can you find yourself in the night sky?

Can you find yourself in both what works for you *and* what doesn't?

Can you find yourself in both your joy and your suffering?

If you can't find yourself in your suffering, you're lost.

If you can't see your reflection in the puddle of spilled tea, you're dead.

So.

Buy a cheap, used, chipped teacup. Fill it with tea.

Hold it up.

Don't miss your life.

SEAMLESS AND ALWAYS FOUND

With form that is no-form,
Going and coming, we are never astray.

It's interesting that the Buddha never taught about meaning.

He taught the origin and cessation of suffering.

That's not meaning. That's an instruction on how to live with greater freedom, compassion, and joy. It's how to hurt less and help others hurt less.

It's interesting that Christ never taught about meaning, either.

He taught people to love: Love all creation and love each other.

That's not meaning. That's an instruction on how to live with greater freedom, compassion, and joy. It's how to hurt less and help others hurt less.

EXISTENTIAL WRESTLING

I was speaking recently at a world religions high-school class. As the 7:30 a.m. first-period students were sleepily and reluctantly filing in, a big senior saw me sitting on a tall stool at the front of the room. (I always feel like a zoo exhibit in those situations, but it's good practice for me.)

The senior asked me, "You're the Zen guy, right?"

I said, "Yup."

"Okay," he quipped, "what's the meaning of life?"

My answer was sudden, and it surprised me as I said it:

"No meaning. Just life."

I liked that student, and I liked his audacity. Sure, he was being a smart aleck and trying to ask the Big Question, but I liked him for doing it. (And I hope he appreciated my equally smart-alecky answer.)

Why don't great teachers teach on meaning or tell us what the meaning of life and the universe is? Why does Zen throw out ideas about meaning as soon as they show up?

Because meaning is too small.

Because meaning, and all its variations, is an ego story. That isn't to say that it doesn't have a place, because it has an important one. But it's still a small place (relatively speaking), and it has limited function because it's ego. Ego is important, of course, and helpful, but ego is also the smallest and most limited part of who we really are.

Think about the times when you've been grabbed by this question. Think about the times you've wrestled with the great existential questions. How were you feeling? What circumstance or experience in your life caused you to ask those questions? How did wrestling with them feel while you were doing it?

When I've asked—even demanded—what the meaning of my life was, I was usually in pain, even despair. For me, *What's the meaning of life?* really meant *I'm scared.*

I'm scared that there's no purpose to my life or to me. I feel fear, despair, hopelessness. I'm scared that I'm unimportant. I'm scared because I feel lost and ashamed and maybe unlovable.

So when I ask for "meaning," what I really want is to be soothed. I want to feel that I matter, that I belong. I wanted to feel seen, heard, valued, loved, never astray.

CONSTANTLY ENTERING INFINITY, NEVER ASTRAY

Never astray is a beautiful idea. *Never astray* makes me feel safe. It sounds like a state of being, a realization of at-home-ness no matter what, no matter where. I've known people like this, people who seem so completely at home in their own skin that they were at home wherever they were. They never seem overly anxious, panicked, or lost. They never seem astray.

I am not one of those people. In fact, I've spent much of my life feeling the polar opposite: I've even felt astray—profoundly astray—while in my own house surrounded by my family.

The variable here is whether or not we feel anchored in the real and connected to ourselves. When small mind (our limited, fear-based ego self) is married to Big Mind (the loving, unbounded consciousness that we most truly are), we are never astray. In fact, when small mind is married to Big Mind, we see that there actually is no *astray*. It doesn't actually exist—it's just a misperception based on a turbulent, and very real, emotional state. When small mind ruins the show, life can feel like an afflictive airport, where *sorrow, anger, lostness, boredom,* and *despair* all take turns arriving and departing, with us helpless to stop them.

In real life, airports can be great. People coming and people going. Leaving old lives and entering new lives. People leaving their homes, bored by travel, world-weary and punched out. People actually running to get to each other just a couple seconds sooner. Reunions and partings, and lots of tears—tears of sorrow at parting and tears of joy at reunion.

In the Narita airport outside of Tokyo, the signs say, *Welcome to World Sky Gate Narita.* How cool is that? Not *airport*, but *world sky gate*! What a poetic way to point out exactly what an airport is. We tend think of airports as "non-places"—places we would only be in if we needed to, lacking personality, soul, or meaning beyond their function. But this term *world sky gate* reminds us that an airport is actually a gate to infinity. Suddenly, the stupid, boring airport is sacred.

The entry to infinity is everywhere.

Of course, saying *entry* only half-works. What is there to enter? Or even to exit? Our non-separateness means never entering anything, never leaving anything. Infinity is never distant. It's closer to you than your own breath, your own thoughts.

WE ARE CONSCIOUSNESS IN BODIES

And yet, without form (matter, physicality), consciousness can't tell when it's rubbing up against something, where its edges are, what it's not. Without form, consciousness can't know itself. Yet form (matter, physicality) without consciousness is just a rock, a tabletop, a pen. Form is how we know consciousness. Consciousness is how we know form. Without consciousness, form can't know itself, either. But when both are present (hello, most life as we know it!), we have both: consciousness in form.

And at the top of the conscious life pile—on this planet anyways—is the amazing human, capable of not only consciousness in form, but self-aware consciousness in form. *We are consciousness in form with the capacity to know that we're consciousness in form.*

And we can then start to see the not-two-ness, the non-separateness, of everything. The *form that is no-form.*

In Zen, we call this the realization of emptiness, or non-self, or Buddha-as-us-and-us-as-Buddha.

The practical, medicinal value of this teaching and realization is actually simple, and not so lofty and abstract as it seems. The delusion of essential separateness gives rise to all sorts of suffering: greed, hate, shame, fear. Those things can't exist without the idea of a separate self informing them. The feelings of being lonely, sad, frustrated, anxious, depressed—all depend on seeing things as "separate."

This is why we can feel lost and lonely sitting on our couch at home, surrounded by family. This is why I can feel at home a thousand miles from home.

But just be fully where you are and there is nowhere else. Home. Never astray.

LOVE MAKES US REAL

Try this: When you're walking around in public, make a stranger a person by thinking to yourself, *I love you* when you see them. Or, at the very least, say, *I see you*. Make your non-places into real places, inhabit your life, make your heart a real heart by saying, *I feel you* to it. See what happens.

Remember *The Velveteen Rabbit*? Its message is that real love makes things real. Love isn't sappy and sugar-coated and Hallmarky and sticky-attached. Love is unconditional, positive regard, and it's the bravest response to life that it's possible to have. Nothing else is even close.

Love makes places real. Love makes us real.

What's the meaning of life? is an incarcerating question.

We only ask it when we're not feeling free. Why would we ask for meaning when we felt we had it? We wouldn't. We don't cry out for water when we're not thirsty. We don't cry out for meaning when we don't need it.

The funny thing is, from a Zen point of view (which is no point of view at all), *What's the meaning of life?* isn't the Big Question.

Because to answer questions about "meaning," to know what "meaning" even is (for you), you must have a point of view, a framework, a starting point, a cultural understanding, a definition. And, generally speaking, as soon as those things try to show up, Zen politely pitches them all out.

All those things are completely personal, relative, and changing all the time. They are all bound by culture and time. So they *can't* be the Big Question, because the Big Question must be timeless, universal, across cultures and ages.

Meaning feels like an opposite of wonder: Wonder feels free and vast, and meaning feels caged—small, tight and limited by its attempts at a narrative and definition of reality.

We're wisely reluctant to posit any assertions about reality. Why would we? Much more importantly, why would we need to?

How do you feel when you feel you need an explanation to understand something? What is that feeling actually telling you? How are you listening to it, and where is it leading you?

When we feel ourselves wanting to posit an assertion about someone, something, everyone, and everything, we should notice that wanting. What is it, really? Where is it coming from? What are our unexamined assumptions and how do they change what we think we're seeing? How are we feeling in this moment that is showing up as an impulse to impose a map on this wild landscape?

The actual feeling, the actual experience of life is lost with too much analysis.

As long as you try to know what life means or why you're here, it is difficult to feel your actual being in this place. And feeling your actual being is your never-astray-ness.

Feel your actual being. That's Buddhism in four words.

THERE IS ONLY HOLY

Plus, *astray* is just an idea.

Think of the most astray moment of your entire life.

Now think of the least astray, most "correct" moment of your life.

Did these two moments not take exactly equal parts in leading you to the exact moment you're in now, holding a book and breathing?

If you look at this closely, you'll see that it's true.

The hardest part of this teaching for us isn't the form-is-emptiness part, or the emptiness-is-form part. *It's holding both at once, each is 100 percent true.*

One isn't 50 percent true and the other 50 percent true. Both are 100 percent true.

We're separate beings. We're not separate beings. Both are 100 percent true at the same time. To lose one is to lose both and lose Reality.

Let's remember that *meaning* is a word that is used and understood in many ways. And trusting that something has inherent value and meaning and needing to know what that meaning is and to measure that value are very different things.

So when Zen says *no meaning*, we're not talking about nihilism. We're not saying that nothing has value or purpose and that life is meaningless and therefore pointless.

We're saying life has all meanings, so it's not limited by any of them.

As soon as we have a meaningful activity, we have meaningless activities. As soon as we have meaningful people, we have meaning-less people.

Meaningful is a personal, subjective, relative value judgment.

And Zen is about tasting the Absolute through the relative. The emptiness through the form, the timeless through the changeable, the holy through the ordinary, the whole through the parts.

If you have meaning, it can be taken from you. It can go away. If only your job makes your life meaningful, what happens when you retire? If only your role as a parent gives your life meaning, what happens when your kids grow up and leave?

But with *no meaning*, nothing can be taken from you. It's all yours. That's what zazen is for: noticing how we attach and how that attach-ment can limit us.

No meaning means that Reality is undistinguished, everything is holy, and there's no place to spit.

No meaning means unlimited. Infinite. It's what my teacher Tim says: "Since all is empty, all is possible."

So let your zazen practice take you beyond meaning. Beyond Buddha, beyond good Zen and bad Zen.

As soon as we attach to our discriminations between good and bad, between holy and mundane, we have war. Just like that.

If you want to stop the war, take care of your shoes.

More accurately, take care of your dancing shoes. No one ever went off to kill someone wearing dancing shoes.

YOUR LIFE IS TOO BIG TO MEAN ANYTHING

The results of our actions and what they "mean" are none of our business. We don't get to know what we actually did, or even if we did anything. In fact, strictly speaking, we have no way of actually knowing the impact we have on the universe, because it's infinite. Our lives are created by every other life in the universe—past, present, and future— and affect every other life in the universe—past, present, and future.

We don't get to know if we're good or not. We don't get to be successes or failures. No seed ever sees the flower. Parker Palmer says:

> When I'm sure I know exactly what I'm doing and why—so sure that I miss vital clues about what's really needed and what I really have to offer—it's a sign that my ego's in charge, and that's dangerous. My best offerings come from a deeper, more intuitive place that I can only call my soul. Embracing the fact that there's no way to know with precision whom or what I'm serving helps free me from the ego's dominion.
>
> All that's in my power are my own intentions and my willingness to give myself to them.

Isn't that freeing? That feels like trusting, but not needing to know.

So the question is, can we rest in our intentions and our willingness to offer ourselves? Can we just do our best to help and stop trying to measure our worth? Can we sit just to sit, and stop trying to measure our progress? Can we love just to love, and stop trying to leave part of ourselves out, to keep it safe, to save it for later?

Our needing to know can be binding: *I can't do anything until I know what it means, I can't travel a road until I know where it goes.*

With thoughts like that, I'm already paralyzed, aren't I?

Zen teaches us that every road goes only to itself. A road is not a means to an end. It's a road.

The point of zazen is to do zazen. It's not a means to an end.

What does zazen do? Nothing! What is it good for? Nothing! What does zazen mean? Nothing!

Zazen is too big to mean anything, just like your life is too big to mean anything. Any story or meaning we'd attach to your life—no matter how big—would just bind it.

If this whole question of meaning is sticky for you, ask yourself these questions:

What do your friendships mean?

What does your marriage mean?

What does the sunrise mean?

What does the face of infinity in the clear night sky mean?

What does a rainbow mean?

What does a piece of string or a magnet mean?

What does a duck mean? *No meaning, just a duck.*

What does a grandmother mean? *No meaning, just a grandmother.*

The actual scope of things repels any attempt to cage them with meaning.

Let's give up the good for the Great, okay? No meaning, just life. When we start trying to find the specific meaning in a specific activity and then rank and gauge the meaning of one activity (or job or partner or religion or diet or, or, or...) against another, we can start to lose it. We can start to think there's a place to spit. And we can start to think that if we don't choose well, maybe *we're* the place to spit. We call that shame. We call it conditional existence. *If I choose the right, good, meaningful things, then I'll be a right, good, meaningful person. Maybe then I'll be okay.*

When we let go of those ideas around meaning that we cling to, even just let go a bit, then we can see that it's actually all meaningful. Life is a mark we can't miss. We still try hard at living life, but that trying isn't rooted in a deep fear of failing or badness, it's rooted in the opposite: loving it all because there's nothing to prove.

JUST TO BE ALIVE IS ENOUGH

Suzuki Roshi once said to someone, "Just to be alive is enough."

Do you believe him?

Probably not. Or rather, your head wants to say *YES*, but the whole rest of your life says otherwise.

Just to be alive is enough.

As a practice, put this book down and really think about that for a few minutes: *Just to be alive is enough.*

Just soak in it a while and notice what arises in your body, your emotions, your thoughts in response to this simple, six-word idea:

Just to be alive is enough.

Anything you notice in yourself in response to this is telling you something important: your ease, your difficulty, your resistance, your longing, your anger, your hope, your contentment, your sadness.

Believing in the niceness of this idea isn't the point. You'll forget that feeling of niceness in a few minutes and go back to misunderstanding everything. You can't talk yourself into contentment. You can learn more from your resistances and arguments about this than you can from your *Oh, that's lovely* thoughts.

So pay attention to the resistances. Where are they in your body? Where are they in your heart-mind? How do you feel when you're resisting? What does that feeling remind you of? How old does that feeling make you feel?

This is a simple exercise, just sitting with a few words and watching the ripples they make when dropped into our consciousness. Everyone's ripples are different, and they are all helpful. They show us where we're healed, and they show us where we're hurt. Then, when we know where we're hurt, we know where our work is to be done.

Just to be alive is enough.

Please stay quiet and still long enough to know what he meant.

To actually know this in your bones would change everything for you forever.

When you allow yourself to dissolve into this moment in zazen, you dissolve into all moments, into *Moment*. There is only one, and you fill it and join with it and *are it* completely. No separation, no gap.

I love the term *moment*, without the modifier *this* or the adjective *present*. Of course it's only moment! What other moment is there, has there ever been, could there ever be?

YOU ARE ALWAYS TOUCHING THE SKY

So. Our zazen is a practice of *non-spitting*, a practice in which there are only places, and never non-places. Zazen allows for and embraces everything. Zazen is a world sky gate: a small place that touches infinity. An infinite place that touches the small. Zazen is a non-place. Zazen is also a place, is also an everyplace. Zazen is also just here, exactly here, only here, now. Infinity. The whole sky.

Duran Duran has a song called "Reach Up for the Sunrise" that contains the intriguing idea that we can touch the sunrise—well, the whole sky, actually—simply by putting our hands up. When you lift your hand—or even when you don't—you're still touching the big, vast, open sky. How can you not?

At what height do you imagine that the sky starts? It doesn't start at 30,000 feet. It starts at the ground. We breathe the sky, turn it into our bodies—along with the rivers and oceans and rocks and animals and plants and the moon and the Big Bang.

If breathing in the Big Bang sounds too weird for you, ask yourself what else could you possibly be breathing in right now? What else even is there?

There is no place to spit.

Every moment touches and suffuses every other moment. Nothing arises alone. Everything arises together—places, people, things, sounds, moments.

Whether or not this place, this moment, is an ordinary one, something to skip over by accident or design, one that's wanting and lacking and non-special, is up to you. Is this moment a place on which to spit?

Where you are, what you see, hear, taste, and touch right now—all of this is your life.

Whether or not this place, this moment is a world sky gate, a real place, a sacred and unique breath, a chance to love, is up to you.

Whether or not your life is sacred is up to you.

Actually, everything is up to you.

THE VOICE

With thought that is no-thought,
Singing and dancing are the voice of the Law.

Part of why I fell in love with my teachers is because of how easily and freely they lived, and how easily and freely they laughed.

Zen has always prized spontaneous joy as an expression of the enlightened mind. Singing and dancing are the voice of the Law, the voice of the highest Dharma. Enlightenment should make us lighter, right?

With thought that is no-thought,
Singing and dancing are the voice of the Law.

Perhaps these two lines, more than any others, are why I trust this Song and the spirit behind it. With this single sentence, the Song escapes being seen as some dead old lecture, dusty and preachy. It can't be dismissed as an expression of boring, fundamentalist, overly religious piety. We instead recognize something that appeals to our youngest self, our highest self, our wisest and most awake self: this life, this path, this Creation, despite its absolute solemnity and stainless, sincere, seriousness, is still ultimately a dance.

AN AWAKENED HEART CELEBRATES BEAUTY

Our vast, collective story is One. And it is a story of awakening, hope, and redemption. It is a song and a dance. Insight, wisdom, and compassion make us *lighter*. That's why we call it *enlightenment*, not enheavyment or endarkenment. An awakened heart is quick to feel it all: quick to cry, quick to laugh. That is understanding.

The enlightened mind is unbound by seriousness. It enters into seriousness without resistance and can abide there with limitless compassion. And it can shed that seriousness like an old snakeskin when it needs to and find again the laughter that comes up from the ground like a fresh spring. It celebrates the beauty that suffuses the universe.

Keats wrote, *Beauty is truth, truth beauty.*

Hakuin wrote, *Singing and dancing are the voice of the Law.* Of course, singing and dancing are expressions of beauty. So, maybe, try on this paraphrase:

Beauty is the Law.

Here's an important Zen truism: Creating beauty is important.

What if the guiding principle, the truth that you followed and led your life by, was beauty? What if you'd vow to do what was beautiful and vow not to do what wasn't beautiful? What kind of life would that lead to?

What kind of thinking makes you feel the beauty of life? What kind of thinking hides the beauty of life? How about speech, action, and livelihood?

What do you say that's beautiful and do that's beautiful? What kind of job would be a beautiful job to have?

As an oft-memed quote says, "If what you said was written on your skin, would you still be beautiful?"

Before you go to sleep at night, asking yourself, "What beauty did I help create today?" would be a pretty good practice for keeping your life on a track you can feel connected to.

Creating beauty is a central human activity and it nourishes a deep part of us. It can express aspiration, hope, connection, longing. Zen centers and temples are famously beautiful, and famously immaculately clean. And the idea here isn't to be OCD and go crazy over cracker crumbs. That's not creating beauty, that's fear. The idea here is to care for things. Caring for things is caring for ourselves, caring for the whole universe.

If you've had yourself some industrial-sized breakthrough experiences in meditation and are careless with your shoes, you haven't yet started practice. This is about living a fully integrated life.

WHOLEHEARTED ACTIVITY IS CREATING BEAUTY

When I see a member of the flower crew at MZMC silently and mindfully creating the many arrangements for the many altars in our center, I am seeing true practice. If someone asks you what Zen practitioners believe, you can point to the vase of flowers on the altar. That would be a good, and deeply correct, answer. (It would also be really opaque and the person asking the question might think your answer makes you really deep, man.)

There's an aesthetic to Zen, and beauty is central to that aesthetic. Anyone who's been on *sesshin*—the formal, traditional monastic Zen retreat expression—knows that it often looks like an elegant ballet: the bows, the prostrations, the bells, the chants, the meal servers entering and leaving the meditation hall with choreographed and graceful precision.

But the Zen creation of beauty is all about honoring the integrity of the moment, of course, and is not focused on leaving an artistic legacy. Tibetan Buddhist monks are famous, like their Navaho American bothers, for creating elaborate, beautiful, and intricate sand mandalas with their hands to aid our insight and healing. Then, when the ritual or teaching is over, the mandalas are simply swept up as any sand might be if it was on the floor and in the way.

The wholehearted and unreserved state of mind while making the mandala is itself the practice. The point isn't the mandala. The point is the making of the mandala. It's the same with the manual labor done in Zen monasteries and on Zen retreats. The point is to do it wholeheartedly, with no part of yourself left out. The point is the state of awareness itself. So we don't sweep to get the floor clean, we sweep to sweep.

Once, at a Brewers game in Milwaukee, I arrived early and watched the groundskeepers prepare the field for the baseball game. It was great, almost like watching altar attendants prepare for a mass in my church when I was growing up.

The best part for me was watching the person whose job it was to draw the lines of the batter's boxes on the sand by home plate. The attentiveness that this was done with was absolutely amazing to me— it was the very same attentiveness I see in the videos of the Tibetan monks and their mandalas. At one point, I saw the groundskeeper get out what was basically a toothbrush in order to get the edge of the white line *exactly* correct.

The reason this was so beautiful to me was my awareness that I was seeing this man's wholeheartedness. No one else was watching him; there was no upcoming judgment or praise or lasting benefit. He knew, as I did, that the very first batter to come up would move the sand and ruin those boxes. The creation took many minutes; the destruction would take a second or two at most. Nevertheless, the lines were created with wholeheartedness and care, without reservation.

In an article about Lady Gaga, the *New York Times*' David Brooks wrote,

> "I suppose that people who live with passion start out with an especially intense desire to complete themselves. We are the only animals who are naturally unfinished. We have to bring ourselves to fulfillment, to integration and to coherence.
>
> "Some people are seized by this task with a fierce longing. Maybe they are propelled by wounds that

need urgent healing or by a fear of loneliness or frag-
mentation. Maybe they are driven by some glorious
fantasy to make a mark on the world. But they often
have a fervent curiosity about their inner natures and
an unquenchable thirst to find some activity that they
can pursue wholeheartedly, without reservation."

To pursue something wholeheartedly, without reservation, is the
heart of Zen and all spiritual practice. And it's not as lofty as it sounds,
because it's not a behavior, it's a state of consciousness, a way of being.

THE SUPPORT OF RITUALS

To help us in this way of being in Zen, we sometimes use *gathas*. A
gatha is a short verse to help cultivate mindful awareness—to change
our relationship with an activity. The Verse Before Shaving that I
shared in Chapter 9 is one such verse. For ordained folks in the Zen
tradition, that gatha is recited, as you might expect, before we shave
our heads.

Head shaving is an ancient tradition, going back to the historical
Buddha's original renunciation of worldly values. After he leaves his
palace and renounces his inheritance, his family, and his throne, he
shaves off all his hair. Now, in the modern secular world, people vol-
untarily shave off their hair for all kinds of reasons, from shocking
their parents to raising money for charity to hiding emerging bald
spots. But within the brutality of the caste system in place in the
Buddha's time, shaving one's head effectively erases them as visible
and viable members of society. We see him go from being royalty to
being a non-person in this single act.

Nuns and monks in many Buddhist traditions still follow this
example and shave their heads at ordination, vowing to live a life of
awakening and non-harm by giving up self-centeredness.

This is one of the great, deep gifts of the Zen tradition: its ritual
elements. What a beautiful way for that Dharma be passed on.

Like most Zen Dharma, this ritual has a physical component (the razor, the act of shaving), a heart-mind element (the verse, the chanting, the emotions), and an expressive Dharma element (the shaven head itself is the teaching, expressing our aspiration).

The shaving is a symbol, a sign, a practice. Some folks use this stuff to their benefit, and some do not. For some, it's supportive and encouraging. For some, it might be an affectation, another trapping for a scared ego to grab onto to make it feel special or important. For me, it's been plenty of both.

Does it help me?

Yes, I think that in the long run, it does. I like my hair. I miss my hair! I want to look good. I want to be cool. So every time I let it go, I'm choosing to let it go again, if only just for that moment. At the same moment, I also see the part of me that wants to stand out, to be seen as special and "spiritual." Look at my desire to be superior and elevated! I bet I know the shame that's trying to cover. So now the ritual of shaving my head has shown me where my work lies. Wow, lots of old suffering there for me to see.

I usually consider my practice to be weak. I usually consider my aspiration to be weak. I consider my doubt to be great and my faith to be great, but my determination to be weak. I don't know if it really is, but the more we practice with honesty, the more we see how we miss the mark. And the more we see that our self-awareness is crucial, but our self-judgment isn't.

What I am saying is that I need help. I need lots of it. So I follow as many of these traditional ways as I reasonably can, because I don't trust my selfishness and blind spots. I know how easily I get blown off course. I know how quickly I'm tempted to betray my path, my values. Yesterday's awareness simply won't do. I need today's awareness, and I'm drawn to see more, feel more, know more today than I did yesterday. So I need reminders and support.

I sometimes long for the ancient ways, but I know I'll never practice that way. It's not possible, nor is it actually desirable, as these aren't ancient times.

But I can try to practice with that same spirit, and maybe feel a connection with those numberless humans who sat like we do, wore clothes like these, chanted this same verse's intention before they chose—one more time—to shave all that hair off, even if it brought tears to their eyes as it did to mine, to aspire to let go of those deep attachments, and to the suffering that they bring.

You can practice in that same spirit too: no head shaving or special clothes required. Use your shower or brushing your teeth as your purification ritual. Light a candle before your daily sitting as an expression of your aspiration to bring the light of your full awareness to everything. Make your meal preparation a sacred activity, ritualizing and expressing your deep desire to create and offer sustenance to a hungry world. Tie your shoes with a heart-mind that says, "I will walk in reverence for all life, and make each of my footfalls on the earth today a grateful kiss on my Great Mother's precious body."

It doesn't matter what the ritual action is; it's a stance of the heart-mind, and you can choose to make the ancient vow your own and get support however you need to get it. Make it personal. Make it yours. Then let go of it being "yours" and just make the vow beyond any limits.

HONORING OUR LINEAGE, HONORING OURSELVES

Once, I was at a Wisconsin Badgers football game at Camp Randall in Madison, Wisconsin, with my wife. One of the things that the University of Wisconsin is famous for is the marching band. They have an amazing band, and they demand very high performance from their members.

The day we were there was marching band alumni day, when past graduates who were once members of the band are invited back to play and march on the field again.

At one point, the current student band was on the field, and stood in long, perfect rows. Then the alumni band was welcomed on to join them. When these old members marched onto the field, the current band all got down on their right knee, placing themselves below the alumni. This gesture of respect, to honor all those who had gone before, moved me deeply. No one needs to be told what that gesture means—they feel it in their chests.

Zazen is just such a ritual.

And like that marching band, honoring all those who have gone before is a huge part of many spiritual traditions.

In the Zen liturgy, we chant the names of the Buddhas who preceded Buddha (all seven of them), then we chant all the names of the teachers and students, starting with Buddha, going all the way up to the present.

It's cool to feel like a non-abstract, direct and immediate participant in all that.

"Those who bear witness to self-nature" refers to all of us who choose to sit down and practice zazen. To sit down and let zazen practice us.

The long line of ancestors, going back to Buddha, and back to the infinity to before, after, and during Buddha.

But on the lineage papers that formal students are given when they receive the precepts and become Zen Buddhists, there's an interesting twist on this too-simple, beginning-to-end idea.

The red lineage line starts with an empty circle that represents the unknowable, unnamable, infinite mystery, then it goes through Buddha, then it goes through his student Mahakashyapa, then through Mahakashyapa's student, then through all the eighty to ninety names of the continuous student and teacher lineage through India, through China, through Japan and America, then down through the student's name at the bottom and back up around the margin of the long page, and all the way up through the circle of emptiness before Buddha, through the Buddha himself. Get it?

It's not a line after all.

It's a circle.

IRRESPONSIBLE ZEN

Orthodox Buddhism has no time for singing and dancing. In fact, singing and dancing are both forbidden, along with a load of other stuff that is associated with distraction and worldly indulgence. From its inception, Buddhism has been a self-described Middle Way between the extremes of asceticism and indulgence. Each sect of Buddhism has its version of what that looks like, and we humans find it very easy to judge where others land on such matters and argue with each other about it.

So *singing and dancing are the voice of the law* is a pretty radical thing to assert, even after Zen had put down deep roots in Japan by the time Hakuin wrote this.

Singing and dancing are still usually seen as variations on the theme of "play" or even "irresponsible screwing around" and practice is seen as practice: upright, sober, quiet, serious.

And it is. Zen is about "the white-hot center of life and death" and that's just true. It's the reason Zen exists. Zen isn't here to make us feel better or try to make us happy. It's here to wake us up. And that's long, hard, damn serious business. But Suzuki Roshi says, *"What we are doing is far too important to be taken too seriously."*

Ahh. Since it's all here, both the important and the unimportant, the terror and the laughter, we must balance the seriousness that's here with the awareness that not-serious, even silly and funny, is here, too.

The entire continuum of human experience, from the lowest lows to the highest highs, is within us. Our work is to not grab the highs and try to own them or reject the lows and try to avoid them. Our work is to be the unceasing, loving witness of the experience as it arises and changes within ourselves. We bear witness to the whole as it manifests in us, and we bear witness with understanding, wisdom, compassion, love.

PRESENCE IS ENLIGHTENMENT

We enter into this life in love with it all: participating joyfully in the sorrows of the world. There is no escape here, no enlightened off-ramp. That no-escape is both wisdom and compassion, both heart-break and joy. And we learn to move so freely between them that there is no effort, only the movement of our awareness.

The witness is so important to maintain because every time we try to grab a high or deny a low, we identify with the constriction of the grabbing and the denying of the very experience we are having.

Our work is to recognize that both denying and pursuing mean that we lose ourselves in the experience. But if we remember to not constrict in response to our experience (either through grasping or avoidance), then we remain in the flow of awareness itself, the wave of *what is*, the peaceful and uninterrupted flow of being. We remain the heartbeat and the breath of the universe. Our practice is to live this realization. We call this kind of living *enlightenment*. And by this point in working with the Song, we should know that this realization is our individual and collective birthright.

We have two basic states: contented and discontented.

When we recognize that we are content, the practice is to be appreciative and grateful. This waters the seeds of appreciation and gratitude and makes them more likely to arise again.

When we recognize that we are not content, the practice is to meet that experience with acceptance and compassion. This waters the seeds of acceptance and compassion and makes them more likely to arise again, like a kind of dance.

KNOWING BEYOND OUR MINDS

Do we still think that enlightenment is mental? That enlightenment is something that we figure out, something that happens inside our skull? Some great cognitive connection that we'll make? Do we think that enlightenment is some intellectual insight that we have yet to have? Why do we think that enlightenment is some amazing cerebral thunderstorm?

As humans, we know in lots of ways. We learn to know with our bodies first.

There's the organ of skin: hot, cold, rough, smooth, touch, separation.

There's the organs and other stuff inside us: hungry, thirsty, muscles contracting and expanding, air coming, air going.

There's what we call "the guts," our intuitive sense: *This person makes me nervous. I should take a right instead of a left. Something's not right here. Something is wonderfully right here.*

Then there's what we call "the heart," our emotional knowing: *I am scared of her and don't feel safe. I love this person. This song always makes me cry. That movie gives me hope and courage.*

Then we have our favorite three pounds, the brain: imagination, thoughts, dreams, ideas, abstract reasoning, rationality, symbols, language.

Wow. That's a whole pile of playgrounds we have at our disposal. But we usually think we're just the last one. What poverty we live in.

Our ideas about our lives are the least true part of them.

Does understanding water help us quench our thirst? No, of course not. Knowing has its place in our life. But to imagine that we've arrived at anything final is misunderstanding. "Final" comes from the same root as "finite," and reality is not finite. Of course, to claim that reality is infinite is also to make a limited claim, so maybe it is best not to say anything.

Maybe it is best to return to silence.

The lyrics to the song "Amazing Grace" speak to the experience of awakening to what was previously unseen, unfelt, unknown:

> *I once was lost, but now am found*
> *Was blind, but now I see.*

These moments of the veil being pulled aside can be quick, simple, and ordinary: "Oops! I'm sorry; I didn't see you there." Or they can be slow and gradual unfoldings—deeply emotional and revelatory. We can call them *aha* moments or even enlightenment experiences. We can experience them as straightforward teachable moments or powerful experiences of grace, conversion, awakening—all filled with unspeakable gratitude, humility, and joy.

So here's what I think is the key to Hakuin's assertion about singing and dancing. It's his caveat, "with thought that is no-thought."

This is what brings us the large pasture beyond form and emptiness, and as Rumi says, "beyond ideas of right doing and wrongdoing."

When we investigate thought in zazen, we find no-thought, or no separation between thought and no-thought. Dogen Zenji calls this "non-thinking" in his essay "Fukanzazengi (Principles of Seated Meditation)."

What are we talking about here? Is it a state of literal not thinking, with no mental activity arising at all? Is that the practice and goal of zazen? Are thoughts the enemy?

No.

I get asked that question more often than any other, and it amazes me how pervasive the belief is that meditation is about developing to ability to stop thoughts.

You don't need to think much when singing or dancing.

ALREADY LIGHT

We're back to the theme of play again. Chanting is singing, dancing is play.

If this practice doesn't make you lighter, at least a little, you're doing it wrong. Get a different teacher or a different sangha or a different practice or quit Zen entirely and take up knitting or the saxophone or riding a scooter. Those can all work pretty well, too, if they're done with devotion and love.

In fact, anything done with devotion and love works. Even Zen.

BOUNDLESS AND BRIGHT

Boundless and free is the sky of Samádhi!
Bright the full moon of wisdom!

Once, on pilgrimage to South Africa to meet Archbishop Tutu and see the Cradle of Humankind, I stood on the shore in the town of Knysna and looked west at the sunset, out over the ocean, toward my home. I felt a longing to be there, instead of where I was, in Africa. The felt experience of longing connected me to my heart, my body, my breath.

And then I remembered that I was already home. Where else could I be? Wherever I live in my body, that is home.

And I was in the place most anthropologists believe is the literal starting point of *homo sapiens*, the original home to all of us. With that shift in perspective, I suddenly felt wonderful. My feet were in the warm sand. The stars were out—tremendously bright there, so far from any light pollution—and the sky was clear. I just stood there and let the experience wash through me. The wind, the cloth against my skin, thoughts, sounds, impulses, all arising and changing and vanishing.

The stars were inconceivably far away, in the most literal sense: I couldn't conceive of the distances I was looking into. Sure, I *knew* that those stars were so many light years away, and their light travels

186,000 miles per second, and blah blah blah. Those labels and symbols could fit in my head, but not the distances.

The breeze caught my robe and it flopped against my shoulder. I held it against my chest to hold it in place as I continued to stare into infinity. My thought that African evening was, *Zen isn't big enough to hold this. Nothing is.*

RIPPLES OF INTERBEING

Boundless and free is the sky of Samádhi!
Bright the full moon of wisdom!

Some wise American Zen teachers chose to borrow the phrase *the sky of Samádhi* from the Song of Zazen and include it in a version of the traditional Zen liturgy where we chant the names of the ancestors, teachers, and students, starting with the historical Buddha and going teacher to student, hand to hand, heart to heart through dozens of generations up to the present, up to all of us in the room, our voices chanting their names, our hot breath bringing those ancient names to vibrant life.

That same section of the liturgy goes on to say: "Our friends and family members guide us as we walk the ancient path. We express our heartfelt gratitude and acknowledge our debt to all successive Buddhas and ancestors who have transmitted the authentic Dharma, including the Great Matriarchs, and we pay homage to the Mother of All Buddhas, Prajna Paramita, and to the first women who realized the Way."

I like the word *suffusion* to describe this interbeing, the nature of reality, time, cause-and-effect, karma, life and death, etc. You know, the usual suspects.

I'll say that to suffuse is "to spread through or to thoroughly permeate," and since everything (and every non-thing) spreads through and thoroughly permeates every other thing (and non-thing), the nature of Reality is *suffusion*. It's another way of talking about fundamental non-separateness. It's *no-gapness*.

There is no space to be found between anything and anything.

We suffer because we forget our inherent connection. Or, more accurately, we suffer because we forget our interbeingness.

Why? Because our tenacious ideas of separation and permanence cause us tremendous suffering. The illusion of separation gives rise to greed, hate, and all manner of afflictions (i.e., grasping, clinging, hoarding, control, possession, competition, desperation, poverty, racism, sexism, nationalism, war, etc.).

Imagine a snapshot of a person laughing while playing cards with her friends. It contains her whole past, the exact and perfect combination of thoughts, emotions, and sensations she was experiencing in that instant, and the photo viewer's awareness that time would march on, their ability to see that instant as an instant in an endless series of instants.

And then we realize that our standing here holding the photo means that we're completely included in that moment, this moment, the one moment, the only moment. We aren't the observers of experience, we are experience. We aren't the observers of moment, we are moment. Integral. Non-separate.

By definition, this most common of moments contains every single other moment. It's perfect. It's timeless time. It's utterly holy, utterly sacred.

What if you were charged with retaking that photo? I love looking deeply into a snapshot and seeing the impossibility of that. The people, the arrangement, the light, the shapes, the shadows, the clothing, the wrinkles, the age of the people, the flow of time.

There is only ripples. That's actually all there is.

These words I type, that you read: ripples.

There is no Dharma beyond this.

THE INFINITE ALIVENESS OF CREATION

Pure awareness—*Prajna Paramita, the Mother of All Buddhas*—leads to an experience that we can call wonder. Wonder is an experience of opening—we get bigger inside. We can include more, and we ache to do just that. When we're in a state of wonder, we immediately feel connected to Something Else, and we immediately yearn to share it, offer it, serve this new connection, this new awareness of our inter-connectedness, of our interbeing.

We can become aware that we're always in front of a live audience.

The entirety of creation is vibrating, is dynamic unfolding, is alive.

We are always in front of that audience of infinite beings, the Cloud of Witnesses, the Buddhas and Ancestors, the Communion of Saints, All My Relations.

All my relations:

Like the trusted and silent simplicity of my tabletop, assembled by someone far away and long gone, made of trees whose roots dove deep into moist black soil and found something there, and above in the open blue heavens, to turn into form.

Like the tabletop upon which rests the slick silver computer, the black keys, the glowing screen, assembled far away in a factory by those human hands attached to memories and hopes and pain, making a few dollars a day.

The slick, silver computer next to which sits my teacup, filled with the last quarter-cup of Iron Goddess of Gunpowder tea, the teacup that used to belong to my grandmother, whose memory still causes my heart to swell and my eyes to fill, who must not be dead in the usual sense of ending. Whose life must somehow still be here, in the curved handle of the cup and this taste of tea, still here in this life, behind these eyes that I vainly and mistakenly call "mine."

"Earthrise" is a photograph of the Earth and parts of the Moon's surface taken by astronaut William Anders on December 24, 1968, during the Apollo 8 mission. It was a recording of the first human sight of the whole Earth as a whole planet.

It's called "the most influential environmental photograph ever taken."

Joseph Campbell said that it was more than that; that it was an irreversible turning point in human consciousness.

It's hard for me to imagine that turning point, since I've only known a world that had already seen this image. But it's easy to see how it captured the collective human imagination and changed—even sub-consciously—how we understand science, religion, and our human species. There's an undeniability about our place in creation in that image, and everyone can close their eyes and see the image of our collective home inside their eyelids.

We can't un-see its—and our—fragility, undividedness, or stagger-ing beauty.

That image was a turning point because it forever erased the idea of an earth-centered universe, and forever erased the solidity of the idea that our human-made borders were real or that we were indeed big and powerful.

We saw it all at *once*. Every single life, every event in human con-sciousness had all happened there—on that little marble. We saw it all, all at once, with our ordinary human eyes. No magic, no tricks, no mystic visions. The entire Earth, right there. It was whole and undi-vided. It was beautiful beyond all possible descriptions, and it defied utterly any ability to describe it.

It evoked wonder, awe, reverence, love, devotion, amazement. It's hypnotic.

The distance between the "religious ecstasy" of St. Teresa of Avila and the Zen student's samadhi experience on the zafu and the soul-piercing awe of an astronaut becomes indistinguishable.

REMEMBER INFINITY

One of my favorite *Calvin and Hobbes* strips shows Calvin and Hobbes standing outside at night looking up at the sky:

Calvin: If people sat outside and looked at the stars each night, I'll bet they'd live a lot differently.

Hobbes: How so?

Calvin: Well, when you look into infinity, you realize that there are more important things than what people do all day.

Hobbes: We spent OUR day looking under rocks in the creek.

Calvin: I mean OTHER people.

By gazing into infinity, we see more clearly what's important. We tend to spend our days pretending: pretending we are separate, creating a fiction of our own grand importance, ignoring uncomfortable realities. And that pretending causes us suffering, like all lies do, so the Buddha prescribed this daily reflection (a chant!) as medicine:

THE FIVE REMEMBRANCES

1. I am of the nature to grow old. There is no way to escape growing old.

2. I am of the nature to have ill health. There is no way to escape ill health.

3. I am of the nature to die. There is no way to escape death.

4. All that is dear to me, and everyone I love, are of the nature to change. There is no way to escape being separated from them.

5. My actions are my only true belongings. I cannot escape the consequences of my actions. My actions are the ground upon which I stand.

This translation, by Thich Nhat Hanh, is the gentlest I could find, but the truth of it still hits most folks like a sledgehammer. Even though we probably don't like this teaching, we cannot argue with it. It's not a list of five beliefs; it's a list of five unassailable truths. And it is not just part of the Buddhist cosmology or worldview. This teaching applies to everyone.

Over the years, I've been surprised over and over again by how foreign-sounding these sentences were for me. I've been surprised by how I consistently didn't like saying them.

I made myself do it aloud each time and not just in my noodle. Somehow chanting a teaching makes it alive in us in a different way than if we'd just read it. And this teaching felt very "body truth" to me—very "in your guts" kind of stuff, so chanting it aloud seemed more appropriate than just reading it silently to myself.

When we step back again and see them as a whole, the Five Remembrances give us some perspective on our lives. This is helpful for providing us some distance from the difficult individual contents of our experience. When we're stressed out because we're in a traffic jam, we can ask: *How will I feel about this situation when I am sick? Old? How much will this matter in three hundred years?*

This teaching is about the fragility of this life, and our true inheritance.

So, before reading further, chant them to yourself, aloud. And as you chant them, pay close attention to your felt experience.

You're back. Thank you. You just added some truth to the world, and you used your own breath and body to do it.

As you chanted, you may have noticed some feelings coming up in you. You may have noticed emotions coming, or maybe tension in your body—maybe, maybe not. Just interesting to note.

Engaging with this teaching is brave work, because for most humans, these are the most fear-inducing facts of our existence.

I really do recommend chanting them daily. And the more time you spend with these, the more they'll whisper a secret into you: *You can stop fighting. Relax. This is good news. This is change. This is what makes everything possible.*

LEAVING BEHIND THE "REFUGE" OF DENIAL

In Buddhism, we "take refuge in Dharma." The truth is supposed to give us refuge and set us free. But at first glance, this Dharma makes us feel the opposite of refuge, and not free at all—we feel exposed, vulnerable, and frightened.

We want instead to take shelter in our usual unconscious denial:

- I can stay young.
- I can stay healthy.
- I won't die.
- The people and things I love most are forever and I will never have to be without them.
- At least SOME of my actions are without consequence—I can get away with this one small crime, this one cut corner, this one ethical shortcut. No one is watching.

Do these beliefs sound familiar? We don't usually hear them in our heads in these clear words, but I think this reflects our operating system much of the time.

We think that these lies protect us, so we cling to them, very naturally. And each of us knows at some deeper level that they actually don't protect us but letting them go is still not easy. Seeing our ignorance is not easy.

I use the word *ignorance* here literally: It's *ignoring*. We're not all stupid or uninformed. We just ignore the truth. We might know it intellectually, but we choose to ignore it, moment after moment. That's why we need reminding.

So. Why do we want the Buddha's antidote to our ignorance, grasping, and irresponsibility? In other words, why are the Five Remembrances important to us?

Because ignoring it causes so much suffering for us. Simple.

By contemplating these facts, we cultivate our spiritual practice. We anchor ourselves in our own right understanding, right conduct and right effort, and our spiritual fetters are loosened and eventually even abandoned.

So let's talk about each of the Five Remembrances briefly:

1) *I am of the nature to grow old. There is no way to escape growing old.*

Already today you've probably used, seen, or been exposed to ads for products specifically designed to help us look younger. Somehow our culture has managed to make us almost believe that aging is unnatural and preventable. Youth is associated with all that is good: energy, stamina, ambition, good looks. And age is associated with being slow, out-of-touch, resistant to change, unattractive. Right?

The funniest part is that once we're born, the only possible alternative to aging is being dead. Yet we still don't like it.

My computer has a calendar program, and when you enter important dates into it, you can set it so the computer reminds you of certain events. I had a birthday recently, and funnily enough, as *I was working on this very chapter*, my computer's calendar popped up its little red alarm clock symbol and it went "DING!" I looked up and read, "Bussho's birthday tomorrow," and I immediately felt sad and a little scared.

Then I thought, *Well, I guess my work with these stupid Five Remembrances isn't done yet!*

So it's helpful to actually say it: "I am of the nature to grow old."

It reminds us that what is happening is not only real, but that it's good. It means we're not dead yet! It's the way of things. We don't have to fight or struggle with it. We can accept and celebrate the flow of our life. We can even explore with curiosity and wonder the changes that come to all of us as we unfold.

2) *I am of the nature to have ill health. There is no way to escape ill health.*

When we become sick, many of us feel that we've done something wrong. We feel we've been careless, or not vigilant enough, or we try to figure out the person who "gave it to us" so we can blame them.

Now, obviously, taking care of ourselves has a huge impact on our health, and living wisely is of benefit to everyone. Things like diet, exercise, and mindful living have a big impact on how often we contract illnesses, and it's good to do these things.

But it's the fact of illness and disease's inevitability that often seems to escape us. We get mad when we get sick. Our first thoughts are often about trying to figure out how it could have happened, and the injustice of being ill. Most of this energy is wasted. Illness is a wonderful teaching, and our lives give us frequent opportunities to slow down and learn these lessons. It's just part of the deal.

3) *I am of the nature to die. There is no way to escape death.*

Oof. This is the biggie.

The inescapable fact of our mortality influences and informs most everything about us. It is the root of much of our fear. In many ways, the unconscious fear of death drives much of what we do and don't do in our lives. It is subtly present at all times, even in our sleep. When I'm explaining the concept of dukkha to people who haven't heard of it before, I say that even if they have no obvious, gross suffering in their lives at present, there is always an unconscious, subtle undercurrent of unease because we all know of our own mortality.

Repeating this remembrance to myself every day has been very instructive for me. I can still feel a visceral resistance to this fact, even after a year of saying it every day.

Imagine our freedom if we didn't fear death. Just imagine!

4) *All that is dear to me and everyone I love are of the nature to change. There is no way to escape being separated from them.*

This is my personal least favorite, and I know I'm not alone.

As much as I hate the idea of my own death, I think I hate the idea of being separated from my loved ones even more.

But every human relationship, without exception, ends with separation (at least a physical one). Separation by circumstance, by choice, or by death. But every single one ends.

After we accept the pretty stark truth of these first four Remembrances, we are naturally going to ask, *What do we have, then? What keeps this from being complete despair? What's the good news?* Or even, *What's the point of anything?*

We can get trapped here if we're not careful and demand these answers before venturing further. Of course, there is no permanent, tangible takeaway "point"—but there is life, love, gratitude, and an infinite number of chances to bring our awareness back to those things. And, perhaps most significantly, to discover what comes after those first four remembrances.

The Fifth Remembrance is just as stark and impersonal as the first four, but it represents the one we can do something about. It's the thing we can actually work with, change, and control: our actions.

5) *My actions are my only true belongings. I cannot escape the consequences of my actions. My actions are the ground upon which I stand.*

This one is the good news, as it were.

And it *is* good news. Our actions have enormous influence on our experience, and we can choose to act wisely and receive the benefits of that wise action.

The Serenity Prayer says, "God, grant me the serenity to accept the things I cannot change, the courage to change the things I can, and the wisdom to know the difference." What we cannot change is the first four of the Five Remembrances. So guess which one gets all our energy? The things we can change: ourselves.

Within this one stubbornly beating human heart are the roots and seeds of a million injustices, a million ignorances, a million wars. And also the roots and seeds of a billion kindnesses, acts of connection, humor.

I've chanted the Five Remembrances before my daily zazen for years now, and after all this time this teaching is still really challenging for me. I like to think that this is a testimony to the difficulty and depth of the teaching, and not to me being a slow learner. But it's probably a bit of both.

IMPERMANENCE IS LIFE

Aging, illness, death, and attachment to what's impermanent: all these cause suffering, right?

The Zen perspective on this stuff includes what we've talked about already, but also blows it all up, too. We have to live in the reality of the Remembrances, but also remember that Reality is bigger than birth and death. It is infinitely bigger.

None of the "good" and "beautiful" things can exist by themselves. Old age exists because of youth. Illness exists because of health. Death exists because of life. Separation exists because of togetherness. There is no separate thing called "life" to cling to, or "death" to fear. Life and death are empty. We cannot actually separate them, any more than we can hand someone just the "heads" side of a quarter without the "tails" side.

As Joseph Campbell says, "Where your pain is, there your life is also."

There your heart is also. Even if it were somehow possible, ask yourself, *What joy could actually come from loving something permanent?* Love by its very nature is someone fragile and impermanent loving someone fragile and impermanent.

Why do we instinctively pick up a flower gently? Because we so clearly see its fragility, its impermanence. We don't pick up a rock that way, do we? We love the flower because it's so fragile. We find it beautiful because it's leaving. Impermanence is the womb of beauty.

With Zen practice, we begin to see the beauty in everything, because everything is leaving.

It is very often the recognition of the fleeting nature of life—its impermanence—that brings people to a deep place. This deep place can be despair. This can be existential ennui or even nihilism. But it can also lead people to deep spiritual practice, as it did for the Buddha. Letting impermanence take us to that place is wise, because, as Fr. Richard Rohr says, "we shouldn't get rid of pain before we have learned what it has to teach us."

It's a good spiritual exercise to ponder with frequency the impermanence of all things. It helps us see our attachments. It helps us disconnect from those attachments and loosen our death grips, if only a bit. It helps us hurt less and appreciate more.

Do this in your own life. For a week, really notice impermanence.

Look for it. Notice impermanence in all arenas of your life: the changing weather, the shifting nature of human connection, the dynamic landscape of sound, and the passing thoughts, emotions, and physical sensations during meditation.

Notice that beautiful heart-shaped design the baristas puts in your latte, knowing that it'll be gone in a minute. Notice how you can make your bed with gentle and attentive care, knowing that you'll sleep in it again tonight. Notice how you create a meal in the kitchen knowing it'll be devoured moments later. Notice how you love someone close to you, knowing that you'll both die someday and be gone like the batters' boxes and latte hearts. *Notice your choosing to do it anyway.*

SEEING THE MORNING STAR

The story of the Buddha's original enlightenment contains a detail I've always found important. It's said that, after meditating all night (at the end of seven days of nonstop meditation), the Buddha awakens—has his first big enlightenment experience—after looking up and seeing the morning star. I like the specificity of this detail, and I like the tenderness that is implied by it. We all know that the morning star is actually not a star—it's a planet. It's a planet that we in the West call Venus. The "morning star" is actually a neighboring planet, one in our own little solar system, a planet named for the goddess of love. Was this part of why this detail was chosen for the enlightenment story? Probably not. That detail was likely included in the story long before we knew about other planets, stars, and orbits, and certainly before Copernicus, Galileo, and a non-Earth-centered understanding of the cosmos, and before and culturally separate from Venus being named Venus. Nevertheless, it's hard to ignore the probably-accidental symbolic significance of the Buddha attaining enlightenment—and thereby changing the course of human history—after seeing with his unaided naked human eyes, a planet essentially named "Love."

Maybe Buddha simply experienced strong affection. Kinship. Personal ties. Warm attachment. Enthusiasm. Devotion. For what?

The whole earth, the whole sky, the whole thing. Him. Her. Them. Us. All of it.

Affection for all of it, personal connection to all of it, devotion to all of it, care for all of it and kinship with all of it. We forget the self that sits zazen. Zazen sits through us, the gap between aspiration, practice, enlightenment and Nirvana disappears. This revelation happens quite naturally, arising organically through experience, experience that less and less is ours, and more and more just is.

Let it all come, let it all flow, let it all be, until it's done.

"This is enlightenment."

THERE IS ONLY *THIS*

When we don't know what Buddha is, *really*, then we need a Buddha.

But when we realize what Buddha is, *really*, then Buddha gratefully vanishes.

> There's no fancy-pants Buddha.
> There's no fancy-pants Dharma.
> There's no fancy-pants Sangha.
> There's just *this.*

And all that's here is this silly, simple, amazing miracle called a human heart, which isn't "a human heart" because it's not separate from anything else in space and time, and "human heart" is too small of a name and too small of an idea to hold all this impossible miraculous manifestation, this thing we vainly call "life," the entirety of creation that humbly and brilliantly arrives as our breakfast of rye toast and butter, as the miles of brilliant flashes of electricity inside us that move hands and fingers, as the rustling noise that a crow's wings make as it drinks from the puddle left in the driveway from last night's rain, as the light from the Big Bang that's still reflected in people's eyes when they watch you walking to your bus after grocery shopping, carrying two bags, as a cup of warm tea.

I often hold and sip a cup of tea while I write. I learned the tea habit from my teachers, and I thank them for it.

I've heard that holding something warm helps people to connect to their hearts and opens them up. Hot drinks demand that we hold them with greater care and drink them more slowly. So we can naturally slow down and take greater care of our lives when we have a nice cup of tea held carefully in both hands.

Our Zen practice is like this too. It's a place where we tend to become naturally quiet, we slow down, and we begin to take greater care of our lives. It's a place to stop for a while and let our lives catch up with us. It's a place to listen and linger, allowing us to truly receive time and all its changing landscapes. We offer to ourselves the gift of moment, and we immerse ourselves in the arising, changing, and departing of the contents of experience, recognizing all of it as not us, and all of it as not separate from us. What a simple, beautiful thing.

Have a cup of hot tea while you read over the next few pages and enjoy the experience of the words and images dancing through your mind, mixing with the taste of your tea.

Are those images, words and tastes separate from each other? Are they separate from you?

You now contain the tea and what you just read. Who are you?

Who will you be when the tea is gone and the book is put away?

13

THIS VERY LIFE

Truly, is anything missing now?
Nirvana is right here, before our eyes,
This very place is the Lotus Land,
This very body, the Buddha.

Over and over, people ask spiritual practitioners, especially contemplative practitioners like Zen students, "What is the use of sitting meditation when there is so much suffering in the world? Why aren't you doing more?"

This is a great question, and I think it always needs to be asked.

In the final stanza of our Song, Hakuin asserts that this very world is the Lotus Land, Nirvana, the perfect place. And we all know that this world is a place teeming with greed, hate, and delusion. It's constantly on fire with continual suffering.

It's easy, especially when we're new, to see contemplative practice as passiveness, detachment, and withdrawal. And since the whole of the Earth is suffering, shouldn't we be doing more than just sitting?

THE GREAT "OUT THERE"

There's a collection of Zen koans from twelfth-century China called *The Book of Serenity* (which is a really great name for a book). One koan in that collection goes something like this:

> Dizang asked Xiushan, "Where do you come from?"
> Xiushan said, "From the south."
> Dizang said, "How is Buddhism in the south these days?"
> Xiushan said, "There is extensive discussion."
> Dizang said, "How can that compare to me here planting fields and making rice?"
> Xiushan said, "What can you do about the world?"
> Dizang said, "What do you call 'the world'?"

There's a lot here, as there is in every koan. And what's here is open to interpretation, like every koan. But for now, our interest is in the first and last lines.

In the first line, we have Master Dizang putting out feelers for where this person's heart-mind is at, where he's coming from. The answer is a physical location, albeit a pretty vague one. That tells Dizang something about Xiushan's state of consciousness: externally focused and pretty literal.

In the last line, we see the master's response to an externally focused, literal question about whether or not his life is doing "enough for the world."

This koan urges me to explore my intentions before I follow them with actions.

Rev. Zesho Susan O'Connell said it this way:

> What is the nature of suffering and what is its ultimate cause? How can I help a world that I see as separate from myself? Wouldn't it be more beneficial for

me to deeply understand how the world is not some-thing "out there" that needs saving? If I consider the way we are all constantly, every moment, making the world then each simple, ordinary action I am able to take right here is "doing something about the world." And when it is time for other kinds of action, less simple or potentially more widely impactful, it is my intention that these actions will be grounded in not knowing what the world is, or what helping is.

This means acting more humbly, with more of an open mind. Perhaps we could rewrite part of this koan to go something like this:

One day Dizang was roller-skating and he fell and skinned his knee on the sidewalk. He was tending to his knee when Xiushan approached him.

Xiushan said, "Why aren't you caring for the world?"

Dizang said, "I am."

Xiushan said, "No, you're not. What about the head? What about the ankles and spine and toes and nose and ear hair? How can you ignore them? You are only caring for the knee!"

Dizang replied, "Right now, the knee is the world."

Perhaps this is a gross oversimplification, but it tries to make the point and it involves roller skates, which are a hilarious invention.

The point is that to turn away from our own suffering is to turn away from The Suffering. And vice versa. Our attention goes to where the suffering is, and we care for it without ownership. To neglect my friend's broken leg in order to first do my meditation doesn't make sense. But to rush out and fix every broken leg at the expense of my meditation also doesn't make sense.

NIRVANA IS NO PLACE—
AND IT'S ALREADY HERE

To refuse to acknowledge, accept, investigate, understand and—most importantly—love our own suffering is to refuse to acknowledge, accept, investigate, understand and—most importantly—love The Suffering—the one and only suffering that is immediate to us, the one suffering that is omnipresent, the one suffering we can *directly* feel and heal. The One Suffering.

There is nothing abstract or distant or later or separate about this suffering. It is already specific, intimate, immediate, non-separate. It is The Suffering, just as much as we imagine others' suffering to be. But if left untended, our personal suffering will prevent us from seeing the suffering of the world and accepting it, understanding it, engaging with it in a way that's actually helpful, actually healing.

There is only heart-mind ("Mind"); our immediate experience.

All we know, or can ever know, is heart-mind.

There is only *one* experience. *This* experience.

There is only either heart-mind ignoring this experience *or* heart-mind meeting and holding it.

So Nirvana is not a place. Heaven, the Lotus land, paradise—not places.

Nirvana is a state of consciousness, a state of heart-mind. It's a state of perfect non-grasping. Appreciation. Complete connection. Not needing anything to be different. The cessation of the fire of suffering.

Does the Nirvana experience last forever? Of course not.

Does anything?

Does the Nirvana experience change us fundamentally? Mmmm, no, probably not. Big experiences can and do change us, but then all experiences do. And as we've already seen, a state of consciousness is not the same as a stage of development. When a ten-year-old's Nirvana experience passes, she goes right back to being a ten-year-old.

After one of my teacher Tim's early breakthrough experiences, Suzuki Roshi said to him, "Now you've had so-called enlightenment. Good. Now take care of your shoes."

Nirvana is never absent, but it doesn't show up the way we expect it to, so we miss it 99.99 percent of the time. So we spend our time killing ourselves.

One of my very favorite teachings of Christ is from the Gospel of Thomas, which reads a lot like a book of Zen koans. I think Hakuin would have agreed with Jesus here because they're saying exactly the same thing: "The kingdom of God is already spread out upon the earth, but you do not see it."

One of our collective, and unexamined, beliefs is that something is missing, that life is broken, that we are lacking, that the world is off-kilter—you get the drift.

So Hakuin is asking us to actually stop and examine these beliefs.

Truly, is anything missing now?

Is it? If you believe that something is missing from your life, from this world, set everything down, sit upright, close your eyes and try to find it.

Try to find this thing that you imagine is missing and you will find only mind. You will find only your imagination, a kaleidoscope of images and ideas and emotions that are creating and sustaining a terrible suffering in you.

Oof.

HOW COULD YOU TOUCH THE WORLD?

So. Out of nowhere, I reach over and I really poke someone on the shoulder.

What will they say? "Ow," they'll say, "Stop poking me!"

Me. Not, "Stop poking the top of my left shoulder!"

I can say I only poked the top of their left shoulder, which is true. But I also poked all of them.

When Buddha touched the Earth to pass his third temptation, we say he touched the Earth, not, "He touched a little spot of ground about the size of a quarter beneath his right knee."

In any given moment, I can ask you, "What are you doing about the world?" but I must mean something specific in that moment.

I might call it "the world," but I actually mean something particular and finite (the particle) or something abstract or distant or generalized (the wave).

"I want to help the world" is a noble and lovely thing to say. You won't get much pushback if you say that to someone. But asking yourself *what that actually means* is perhaps even a nobler and lovelier thing.

Starting with not knowing the answer to that question is deeply wise. We call this "Don't Know mind" in Zen, and the whole world could use a healthy dose of it, you and me included.

Don't Know mind isn't anti-intellectual, nor is it a praise of ignorance. Instead, it's a profound and humble starting place to any inquiry. We start our profound inquiries with a wide-open pasture. The pasture of not knowing.

With practice (zazen!) you can adopt Don't Know mind about what *the world* actually is, and what *help* actually is.

You can adopt Don't Know mind about *where* the world is. (Is it inside of you? Outside of you? Both? Neither?)

You can adopt Don't Know mind about your helpful ideas for the world. Where did your ideas actually come from? What is an idea? What is a thought? What is a thought made of? Can you think without language? Are thoughts in English? Can you think without images? What if you were blind?

If your ideas and your thoughts are yours, why can't you stop thinking? Why can't you stop the song stuck in your head? When you have ideas you don't want to have, why can't you stop yourself? When you get what you imagine is a great idea, where did it come from? Is it yours?

You can see that this can lead to a paralyzing rabbit hole. But I hope you can also see that it can lead to a very helpful deconstruction of what we assume is going on about our actual motives, actions, and their consequences. This is so important. Why? *Because so much of what we think is "helping" isn't.*

Our Don't Know mind is very important here:

Me thinking I know what you need is very dangerous for both of us.

My country thinking it knows what your country needs is dangerous.

My gender thinking it knows what yours needs is dangerous.

My race thinking it knows what yours needs is dangerous.

"Don't know" is especially important when I deeply consider, *Why do I actually want to help?*

My thoughts are connected to my emotions and my emotions are connected to my thoughts. My feelings and thoughts are a product of past causes and conditions. My past karmic conditioning is what gives rise to the emotions and thoughts of this moment.

So to not investigate, understand, or ask about our interior state is to be flying blind. Autopilot. Robot. Zombie. And then we hurt ourselves and each other.

Back to helping the world. Here's another retelling of the koan we started this chapter with:

> In the middle of Lake Helen, one wave asked another, "What are you doing to help the lake?"
>
> The second wave replied, "What do you call, 'the lake'?"

Or even:

> One wave sees another wave helping itself and says, "Stop helping the lake! Mind our own business!"

Waves are the lake and the lake is waves. (Or, as Zen folk love to say, form is emptiness and emptiness is form.)

The world's suffering is your suffering and your suffering is the world's suffering.

If I trace my personal suffering back far enough, I get to all humanity. I get to you. I get to The Suffering.

Howard Thurman, in his 1980 commencement speech at Spelman College, said,

> I can become quiet enough, still enough, to hear the sound of the genuine in me. I can become quiet enough, still enough, to hear the sound of the genuine in you. Now if I hear the sound of the genuine in me, and if you hear the sound of the genuine in you, it is possible for me to go down in me and come up in you. So that when I look at myself through your eyes, having made that pilgrimage, I see in me what you see in me and the wall that separates and divides will disappear and we will become one because the sound of the genuine makes the same music.

Although Howard Thurman was a Christian, this passage perfectly describes the Zen Buddhist understanding and relationship with suffering.

If you go into your own suffering all the way, you'll find the suffering of others. Then you'll find love.

INHERITING THE ENTIRE EARTH

When I was born, I inherited my grandfather's violent alcoholism and my grandmother's tender artist's heart. I inherited Harriet Tubman and Hitler, Gandhi and Pol Pot and Sojourner Truth and my next-door neighbor.

So did you.

I inherited Mara's deceptions and Buddha's enlightenment.

I inherited Pontius Pilate and Mary, the mother of Jesus of Nazareth.

A big part of our karma, our literal physical inheritance as humans, is given to us and grown by us in the womb. It's part of the template.

Our cellular memory is both personal and collective. As American neuroscientist Candace Pert wrote, "The subconscious mind is really the body. Peptides are the biochemical correlate of emotion."

Once we're born, it's too late: We inherit the whole earth.

When I was born, I didn't just inherit that hospital bed. I didn't just inherit the hospital. I didn't just inherit Golden Valley, or Minnesota, or the US.

I also inherited my parents' karma: their genetic tendencies, their eye color, skin color, bone structure. And it didn't stop there.

I also inherited my parents' parents ... and my parents' parents' parents.

And my ...

And my ...

I inherited *human*.

All of it. All the "good" karma, and all the "bad."

When I was last in South Africa, I visited a place called Maropeng, near the Sterkfontein caves where the earliest *homo sapiens* were found. There's a natural history museum there that talks about the origins of our species. Outside there's a sign that says, *"We are all African."*

If I trace my personal DNA ancestry back far enough, I get to Ireland and England and Germany and Scandinavia. If I trace further, I eventually get to Africa, like we all do. All our history is shared history.

This also means that cause and effect are both relative (linear) and absolute (non-linear). Not only are we informed by our past, but we can also change it. Those patterns that create us are not locked in the past. They're in our bodies and minds now, which means that when we access and heal them, we're healing the past in a very real way.

Thich Nhat Hanh says it this way: "When we touch the present moment deeply, we touch the past; and if we know how to handle the present moment properly, we heal the past."

HEALING THE EMBODIED PAST

Recently, in an effort to help heal a herniated disc, I had a subdural steroid injection into my back between the vertebrae of my spine. I expected this to be an experience to be endured. I didn't expect it to teach me anything. But it certainly did. (It's amazing how much we miss when we decide that something is to be endured, not experienced, embraced, and explored.) Here is what happened:

After changing into the backless gown and being escorted down a long hallway, I walk into the procedure room and see the specialized table and its crinkly paper cover and head-holder. There is a big crescent moon-shaped machine that extends a scanner above my body, and the nice technician changes into a thick, lead apron-dress to shield herself from the radiation.

I am suddenly aware of being very scared. I am aware of the raw vulnerability of being placed facedown, and it is startling to me. I begin to break out in a cold sweat. As the first of two injections is administered, my heart begins to race, and I am overtaken with a vague yet pervasive nausea.

At this point, the technician asks me how I'm doing. Before thinking about it, I say, "Great! No problem!"

Five minutes later, the procedure is over and she's walking with me back to the changing room, and soon after I'm alone in a little room, changing back into my normal clothes.

I am then suddenly aware of being sad, angry, and scared, all at once. I notice wanting to cry, and without thinking, I talk myself out of it in about two or three seconds:

No, this is not real trauma. So this is not real fear. You're done, it's over, so go home.

Another fifteen minutes later, I'm alone while waiting for my ride home, and I finally choose to allow those feelings to arise and wash through me. I choose to allow the kaleidoscope of physical impressions and emotions do their dance, allowing them to arise, change, and leave without interpretation, analysis, or judgment.

I start to make connections about what just happened. I could actually, physically feel how the fear and trauma of that little collection of minutes during the treatment was suppressed and funneled into my body, arising later when I was alone. I had been sad, angry, and scared in response to that procedure. But before even registering those feelings, I instinctively suppressed my experience for the assumed benefit of the two other people in the room, the tech and the doctor. *I gotta hold it together in order take care of these two powerful people,* I may have thought.

In real life, I'm a grown adult in a safe place being cared for by two safe, grown adults. There is no need for me to caretake them or in any way be deceptive about my experience. Yet I did both of those things before thinking about it. Like so many of us, caretaking is my default setting. If not actively paying attention, I'll always defer to that.

I denied my experience by repressing it in order to care for the feelings of the two people in charge in the room, one male and one female. You don't have to be Freud to figure this out.

Two weeks prior to my injection procedure, I had visited my massage therapist to help with the pain. I've worked with her for years and trust her completely. At one point during that appointment, she held my head and asked me to release it into her hands, to release the muscles holding it up. I couldn't. No matter how I tried, I couldn't. *You're okay, you're safe, we trust her,* I told my body. No dice. The truth of my injury was that I was too vulnerable, too weak, too hurt. The trauma stored in my cells couldn't be fooled or overridden. It was matter over mind.

Trauma specialist Bessel A. van der Kolk says, "As long as you keep secrets and suppress information, you are fundamentally at war with yourself. The critical issue is allowing yourself to know what you know. That takes an enormous amount of courage."

Bad stuff happened to you years ago. I can say this with certainty because bad stuff happens to everyone. And when that bad stuff happened, you cried out some of that bad, and the rest you put into your body.

We don't know we're doing it, but we do ask our bodies to absorb and hold a tremendous amount—grief, anger, confusion, violence. Once we know this, we must enter into a peace treaty with our own too, too solid flesh. *Ahimsa* ("non-harm") is at the core of Buddhism, indeed at the core of all true spirituality, but we rarely extend it to ourselves—emotionally, mentally, or physically. We perpetually leave ourselves out of the kindness equation.

But our *ahimsa* toward ourselves is our primary project. It's nothing less or other than how the universe treats the universe. To treat something (like our bodies) kindly in hopes of improvement isn't actually compassion, it's a control tactic. We want to change something, to control how it shows up. To treat something with kindness simply because it is and it hurts is compassion. Is love. Is enlightenment.

BEAR WITNESS, STOP VIOLENCE

Let's vow together to treat all beings—including our faithful, hurting bodies—with only kindness.

What you didn't have years ago, when you were pouring out your heart, was a stable and loving witness. Back then, it was just the pain, just the expression of that pain. Your pouring out, your offering, was so pure, so utterly beautiful. You were crying, *Help me!* And now you can respond. You can pick up that phone that's been ringing for all these years, with a sobbing you on the other end, still making the call, still reaching out. *Your reaching is the connection, your answering is the connection.*

That call is happening *now*, and your answering is *now*. So you can hold your past self. Do it. You are her, now, and you are the stable, loving witness that she's always needed. Call it compassion; it is. Call it communion; it is. You're literally reclaiming yourself.

The First Noble Truth of Buddhism is, *We are all in pain. We are all suffering.* In response to this truth, we have choices. We can deny. We can try to run away. We can repress, suppress, analyze, distract, numb, amuse, ignore. Many of us do. Most of us do.

And we can do something else: we can choose compassion. Bearing compassionate witness heals suffering. Nothing else does.

The hard truth is that our wounds are our wounds and our suffering is our suffering. If traditional Buddhism does nothing else, it at least insists that we take care of our own pain. It places the responsibility for our suffering squarely where it belongs: on us, as individuals. And as helpful, and occasionally even necessary, as hope and dreams of a better tomorrow are, they never change our responsibility for healing and the fundamental place of that practice and transformation: this very heart-mind, this very moment.

Bearing witness to peace is easy. That's the most comfortable zazen.

Bearing witness to grief, loneliness, greed, hate, selfishness ... is not easy.

It is hard to bear witness to war with a peaceful heart.

I want to stop the war. I want to end the conflict. Since I know that adding anger to anger doesn't help, I want to stop the war with "peaceful intervention."

If I want to do "peaceful intervention," where is the peace I want to intervene with?

We can call this bearing witness. Or we can call it zazen because that's what zazen is. Zazen is the awakened heart sitting undefended inside the joyous and suffering world, knowing it all as just itself, and knowing all of itself as the just the world. When you sit zazen, sit this way.

How many witnesses does it take to stop violence?

One.

Violence is born in the human heart-mind. If one person—the person whose heart-mind it is—bore witness to the seeds of violence in their own heart, with acceptance, curiosity, kindness, love—the violent act wouldn't happen.

Ripples are real. Consciousness is contagious.

The awareness required to investigate this in our moment-to-moment experience is very subtle, so our awareness must become very subtle, too, in order to see it. To watch and feel the creation of suffering in the heart-mind is miraculous. When we see exactly how we create dissatisfaction, we see how to stop. We see that the state of our heart-mind before we create that dissatisfaction—our natural state—is its opposite: satisfaction. Contentment. Simple awareness, dynamic, luminous, transparent, brilliant. Arisings like fear, greed, and misunderstandings are *extra*. They're weather. And being weather, they are (a) inevitable and (b) always, always passing, leaving behind them a perfect, open, peaceful sky. Each time, every time.

We simply arrive home, again and again, the place we never left, the place it's impossible to leave. Bingo bango. Home again, home again, jiggety jig.

HARDWIRED FOR COMPASSION

When you were a kid, you roller-skated until you fell and skinned your knee. Without thinking, you reached for it, touched the wound with careful attention, and you held it. You did this because you are hardwired to do this. You are hardwired to reach for suffering and care for it. Before you think, before your ideas, before anything, before there's even a "you" and before your ideas of "I" and "wound" and certainly way before your fancy ideas of "being good" or, heaven forbid, "compassion."

You do this because it's your nature.

Kwan Yin, the symbol of perfect and universal compassion in Buddhism, is sometimes depicted having dozens, or even hundreds, of hands, each with an eye in its palm. It's a strange image to some of us, but the image is designed to symbolize the vast capacity that we each have for compassion: to see and meet suffering with tenderness, wisdom, and care. We are all Kwan Yin.

"Which means all of reality is love, love that accepts suffering. To say that love or compassion is something extra, something particular, some admirable feeling or impulse, is good, but it misses this crucial point about life," Norman Fischer said.

Compassion is your nature. Compassion is The Nature. It's the nature of your consciousness.

Make your life into this. Make your life into one big teaching for the wounded, the hurt, and caring for it. That's all.

It's actually that simple. Not easy, but simple.

There is no Dharma beyond this.

REMEMBER

In my years of relationship with the Song of Zazen, I've often wondered what moved Hakuin to write it. Unlike many other Zen verses, it's not strictly just a teaching or collection of teachings. Sure, there's teaching in it and it offers us some metaphors and outlines some ways of understanding zazen and its place in the Zen tradition. But this song seems impatient with the party line, no matter how lovely and lofty it is. It seems to want to break out of church and do cartwheels on the lawn, chase soap bubbles, make faces with kids, kick a red rubber ball as hard as we can just to see it fly.

My felt sense of this song is that it's less about teaching us something and more about singing. It really does feel to me like an expression of deep devotion gratitude, an ode of praise, a (calculated and careful) yelp of deep joy.

It's a love letter.

WHY DON'T WE DO MORE OF WHAT HELPS?

Writing a love letter is a brilliant act. It's an impulsive and mad attempt to do something inherently impossible—describe a huge and deep feeling, a response to the universe in a specific and unique human form. We should all spend a lot more time writing love letters. And not just to our romantic ideals, but to all that we love:

parents and kids, neighbors and coworkers, sunsets and warm blankets and cats and sets of house keys and hot showers and welcome mats and chocolate bars and dandelions and cups of tea and small motorcycles.

When did you last write a love letter?

That's too long. Put this book down and write one, then come back when you're done.

You're back? Good.

How do you feel now compared to a few minutes ago?

If cultivating warm and helpful and intimate and appreciative and grateful and connecting feelings is that simple, why don't you do more of it?

This isn't just me being impertinent and annoying. It's actually a good question. Why don't we do more of what helps? Why do we pretend art is hard? Why do we think happiness is so damn elusive, when it's so obviously not? Why do we feel unsupported when the entire vast Earth is exactly beneath our feet every instant of our entire lives? Why do we feel stuck when our experience is changing from instant to instant every moment, forever?

Sitting zazen helps us to explore these landscapes.

So, now that we're done reading the Song of Zazen, we can finally begin.

What should you do with all of this? What should you do with all that you've read here?

Don't do anything with it. Forget all of it.

Zazen seems to get more mysterious over the years of our practice. We seem to understand it less and trust in it more. People whose lives have been expanded, lightened, transformed, and illuminated from within by this simple practice can't help but feel a deep gratitude and devotion to the practice expression that helped free them from the tyranny of ideas, thoughts, and the netted cages of belief. It feels natural that we try to express our love and to encourage others to take the same medicine that did so much for us.

But what I think about the Song doesn't matter. The Song is long dead.

Long dead, that is, until you resurrect it by investigating it yourself. How?

Chant it every morning for a year after your zazen.

If you don't chant already after your zazen, start.

If you don't sit zazen every day, start.

"Just keep lighting the candle," as Abbot Shoken Winecoff Roshi says.

No excuses, just do it. Be a disciple of your own truth, your own life.

BE HONEST, AND BEGIN

The word *discipline* comes from *disciple*. What are you a disciple of? What are you following, really? Most of us, if we're fearlessly honest, don't like our answers: Comfort. Pleasure. Distraction. Escape. Illusion.

In an AA meeting once, someone said, "My drug of choice was 'MORE.'" I knew exactly what she meant, and her comment pierced me to the center. I hadn't had a drink in a long time, but after her comment, I knew my recovery wasn't finished, not by a long shot. I still prayed at the altar of MORE every day, still belonged to the cult of busy, of acquisition, of distraction, of illusion.

This realization is where Buddhism starts. It recognizes that we all do this to some extent and that we suffer as a result. It offers us a prescription to ease and transform our suffering, but we resist it. The sad truth is, we mostly prefer our dis-ease to its cure. So we orbit our spirituality, our meditation practice, our inner landscapes, and we drop in when it's convenient, when we want to think of ourselves as (or be seen as) "spiritual," or when it might feel good.

We orbit and we dabble in the cure, so of course we don't improve much. The practice at the core of your life is just one of several hobbies, and we pick it up and set it down when it suits us.

And you know what? That's fine. It's better than no practice at all. It's only about 2 percent better, but it's something. And the hope is that when the shit hits the fan and our suffering goes from an irritant to overwhelming, we might remember our prescription and actually take it.

I might resist it sometimes, or it might take some working with before I open to it fully, but Truth supports us. It heals and informs our lives when we let it. So we can trust the Truth of these teachings. We can let them clear our heads about life's priorities. We can let them soften and open our hearts, even if it hurts a bit. That's okay. That pain is where our life is. That pain can open, and compassion can arise in us when we see others' suffering as our own. And then we're not scared. We just want to help. And it's all clear. And it's all okay. The fact that we can face and transform suffering is what makes it okay.

That's why I believe that compassion is the greatest energy there is. It transforms the ground of all suffering—fear of suffering itself—and insists upon evolution. Compassion is the antithesis of fear, hate, greed. *Compassion is the evolutionary impulse of consciousness itself.* It changes us from the inside out and it will not tolerate leaving anything or anyone behind. It is the essence of the Four Bodhisattva Vows, the essence of Zen Buddhism, the essence of the human animal. It's good kung fu. And if you practice it, *really practice it*, it will save you—the only person you can save. And that's who you always have to start with: yourself.

JUST KEEP LIGHTING THE CANDLE

So. Meditate. Sit zazen. Find ways to pay deep, kind, close attention to your inner life. Do it out of great love, or out of great longing for freedom. Or both.

Don't sit out of fear or the desire to be good to get anything, especially not enlightenment. Zen teacher Brad Warner said, "Enlightenment is for sissies" and I'm thrilled that he said that. Seriously. That's solid Dharma, damn good, museum quality. Don't sit for your stupid enlightenment. That's way too small a reason. Sit for the sake of all beings. And remember that you're one of them.

Or ignore me and go ahead and sit just for yourself. It actually doesn't matter. Because if you're truly sitting, it ends up being for all beings anyway. Trick yourself, if you need to, but get your butt on the cushion.

Just get up a little earlier, light a candle, offer some incense, sit zazen, chant the Song, and then go about your day.

And, if that doesn't feel like enough to you and you're itching to do more, then relax and pay attention. Relax your agenda and desire to control. Bring some peace into your life by relaxing your shoulders and deepening your breath down into your diaphragm. You're alive. Pay attention to what's happening. What do the movements of the world trigger inside you? Can you meet what arises with curiosity and care?

Just do the practice. Instead of not noticing, notice. Instead of sleeping, wake up. Instead of forgetting, remember. Relax, and pay attention. Just keep lighting the candle. Just keep lighting the candle. Just keep lighting the candle.

There you go. Now you have something to do, a world to hold with compassion, a past to heal, a future to offer hope to. All by yourself, right now.

You cannot fail. It is always done. Because yes, your life is a mess. You need some improvement. But you're perfect as you are. And this very life, this very body isn't just okay, or even good enough. It's Buddha.

Please don't ignore it, don't be unkind to it, don't underestimate it. Please don't miss it.

APPENDIX

ZAZEN INSTRUCTIONS

When beginning our zazen practice, whether on a meditation cushion, in a chair, or on a bench, we begin by pulling our attention in. We allow our usual concerns, plans, to-do lists, past and future to be temporarily set aside, and we bring our attention as fully as possible into the present and immediate moment.

We begin to feel the support of our posture, connecting us to the solidity and support of the whole, still earth. We become aware of our balance and the upright, dignified, and long spine.

We notice the balancing of the head on our neck and shoulders, without strain or great effort.

We tuck our chin in slightly, resting the tongue behind the teeth at the roof of the mouth.

We relax our face, and let our shoulders drop a bit away from the neck. We leave our eyes partially open, with a soft downward gaze about three feet in front of our seat.

Now we form the cosmic mudra by resting our left hand upon our right in our lap, thumbs gently touching, as if holding all of creation in that beautiful shape.

Our attention can now gently rest in the sensations of the body and ride the waves of the breath, through the natural, unforced in-breath and through the easy out-breath. We can notice anything present, arising within and without.

If our mind is particularly busy or drowsy or scattered, we can count each exhalation, one through ten, then starting over.

When our mind inevitably becomes lost in memories of the past, imaginings of the future, or a fantasy, we simply notice and gently acknowledge this, and without self-judgment, bring attention back to the breath, each time beginning again, knowing that each time we become aware of our mind being somewhere other than here and now, this is the real practice, the moment of waking up to the present, as it is.

Sometimes, if we have been practicing zazen for a long time, resting attention in the breath may feel less necessary for attention to remain stable and present. And we may find our attention spontaneously broadening, resting in the wide field of awareness itself, noticing whatever arises in this moment. This is called *shikantaza*, or "just sitting," in open awareness. But this is nothing special, and we needn't be concerned if it naturally happens or not. Either way, our practice is just to sustain our awareness on what is here with kindness and curiosity.

We do not strive to stop thinking or for a blank mind—this is not the goal of zazen. Presence is the goal of zazen.

It is natural for our brains to create thoughts, images, feelings, and other mental formations. That is simply what brains do. When, in providing instructions for zazen, Dogen writes, "Think non-thinking," what he means is to not chase after or pursue discursive thought.

When, in zazen, we find that we have become caught up in discursive thought, we simply notice it. No problem. We simply and gently acknowledge what is and, without judgment, return to the breath. Our relationship to anything that arises is always one of kind curiosity.

These are the basic steps to build up our capacity to "relax and pay attention." When we have honed our ability to notice when we're paying attention and when we're letting our minds wander or our thoughts to loop back on themselves, we can begin to investigate what we notice. We may be able to say, *Oh, I keep coming back to the thing my partner said to me this morning. Why does that have a hold on me?* And then we sit with the question and we notice. We notice what comes up, and what's under that. And what's under that, and under that. (See Chapter 8 for some specific examples of what this might look like.) We become able to see and hold multiple layers at the same time.

> *When even just one person at one time sits in zazen,*
> *They become, imperceptibly, one with each and all of*
> *The myriad things, and permeate completely all time,*
> *So that within the limitless universe, throughout past,*
> *Future, and present, they are performing the eternal*
> *And ceaseless work of guiding beings to enlightenment.*
>
> *Only this is not limited to the practice of sitting alone;*
> *The sound that issues from the striking of emptiness*
> *Is an endless and wondrous voice that resounds*
> *Before and after the fall of the hammer.*
>
> *You should know that even if all the buddhas in the Ten direc-*
> *tions, as numerous as the sands of the Ganges River, together*
> *engage the full power of their*
> *Buddha wisdom, they could never reach the limit, or*
> *Measure, or comprehend the virtue of one person's zazen.*
>   —from "Jijuyu Samadhi" by Dogen-zenji

THE EIGHTFOLD NOBLE PATH

The Eightfold Noble Path functions as the Fourth Noble Truth. It's the Buddhist prescription to transform suffering in our lives so that we can help transform the suffering in the lives of others. It's comprised of Wise View, Wise Aspiration, Wise Speech, Wise Action, Wise Lifestyle, Wise Effort, Wise Mindfulness, Wise Concentration. It can be helpful to see the eight steps having three sections: *wisdom* (Wise

View and Wise Aspiration), which is essentially an understanding of how suffering arises in our heart-minds and a resolve to consciously work with it; *ethics* (Wise Speech, Wise Action, and Wise Livelihood/ Lifestyle), which is essentially about behaving in the world in a non-violent manner, acknowledging our interdependence; and *meditation* (Wise Effort, Wise Mindfulness, and Wise Concentration), which are the three inner components cultivated in formal meditation and in ongoing, everyday self-awareness.

Rather than a checklist of accomplishments or a list of rules to fol-low, the Eightfold Noble Path is perhaps best understood as a basic recipe for actively cultivating an aware, compassionate, and wise life. And because we are infinite beings with infinite aspiration, so our work with our spiritual path is wonderfully endless.

MORE ON CHANTING

I refer to chanting practice in this book and I tend to forget that not everyone is familiar with it.

Chanting in the Soto Zen tradition is exceptionally user-friendly, as it's almost always done on one single pitch, and some (like the Heart Sutra) are done accenting the syllables, so even if you've never heard a passage or scripture before, you have a pretty good chance of reading along in a chant book and figuring it out in real time.

Chanting is just singing, so everyone can do it. Chanting is usually simpler and easier than singing, that it has a smaller melodic range and asks less of our sometimes-tone-deaf ears. Like singing, chanting awakens both hemispheres of the brain, so it's a great way to encoun-ter something with more than just our logical and rational sense. Every tradition has some variation on chanting, often several, and often blurring the line between what we'd usually consider chanting and singing: Kirtan, Gregorian, Benedictine, mantra, the Psalms, rosa-ries, evensong, taize, etc.

For example, the first lines of the Heart Sutra are chanted on a user-friendly pitch that most voices can match—pretty close to a standard speaking pitch.

Choose your note and stick with it, no rises, and no falls. Just sing the syllables at a regular pace:

"A-va-lo-kit-ish-var-a Bo-di-satt-va, when deep-ly prac-ticing pra-jna pa-ra-mi-ta, clear-ly saw that all five agg-re-gates are emp-ty and thus re-lieved all suff-ering."

It can almost sound robotic, but again the idea is to find the rhythm in the syllables and memorize them. To give you a rough idea of speed, the Heart Sutra usually takes about three minutes to chant at my temple, but that speed can vary quite a bit. And when you're just doing this alone at home, who cares how fast or slow you go? Play with it and find what feels good.

Hearing this done can be helpful, so check out some variation on "Zen Chanting" or "Heart Sutra chant" on YouTube and you'll hear what others do.

For more on Zen chanting, you can check out the book *Chanting from the Heart* from Thich Nhat Hanh and the Plum Village community, as well as the companion recordings, "Chanting Breath by Breath."

This Zen chanting technique means you can chant anything. No melody or skillset or cleverness necessary. If you're struck by, moved by, or puzzled by a poem or passage from scripture or a favorite book, chant it for a while and see what shows up. I promise that it will shift for you and become more than what it was when you just read the words in the page.

Hearing the sounds of the symbols we call words is important, especially the sound of words we consider wise, loving, or in any way sacred. And hearing them in our own voice, formed from the breath coming from inside our own warm and living bodies is an intimate relationship with words that, through repetition, become increasingly ours.

HEART OF GREAT PERFECT WISDOM SUTRA

Avalokiteshvara Bodhisattva, when deeply practicing prajna paramita, clearly saw that all five aggregates are empty and thus relieved all suffering. Shariputra, form does not differ from emptiness, emptiness does not differ from form. Form itself is emptiness, emptiness itself form. Sensations, perceptions, formations, and consciousness are also like this.

Shariputra, all dharmas are marked by emptiness; they neither arise nor cease, are neither defiled nor pure, neither increase nor decrease. Therefore, given emptiness, there is no form, no sensation, no perception, no formation, no consciousness; no eyes, no ears, no nose, no tongue, no body, no mind; no sight, no sound, no smell, no taste, no touch, no object of mind; no realm of sight, no realm of mind consciousness. There is neither ignorance nor extinction of ignorance, neither old age and death, nor extinction of old age and death; no suffering, no cause, no cessation, no path; no knowledge and no attainment.

With nothing to attain, a bodhisattva relies on prajna paramita, and thus the mind is without hindrance. Without hindrance, there is no fear. Far beyond all inverted views, one realizes nirvana. All buddhas of past, present, and future rely on prajna paramita and thereby attain unsurpassed, complete, perfect enlightenment.

Therefore, know the prajna paramita as the great miraculous mantra, the great bright mantra, the supreme mantra, the incomparable mantra, which removes all suffering and is true, not false. Therefore, we proclaim the prajna paramita mantra, the mantra that says: *"Gate, Gate, Paragate, Parasamgate, Bodhi, Svaha!"*

THE FIVE REMEMBRANCES

1. I am of the nature to grow old. There is no way to escape growing old.
2. I am of the nature to have ill health. There is no way to escape ill health.
3. I am of the nature to die. There is no way to escape death.
4. All that is dear to me and everyone I love are of the nature to change. There is no way to escape being separated from them.
5. My actions are my only true belongings. I cannot escape the consequences of my actions. My actions are the ground upon which I stand.

SANDOKAI (THE HARMONY OF DIFFERENCE AND SAMENESS)

The mind of the great sage of India
  is intimately transmitted from west to east.
While human faculties are sharp or dull,
  the Way has no northern or southern ancestors.
The spiritual source shines clear in the light;
  the branching streams flow on in the dark.
Grasping at things is surely delusion;
  according with sameness is still not enlightenment.
All the objects of the senses
  interact and yet do not.
Interacting brings involvement.
  Otherwise, each keeps its place.
Sights vary in quality and form,

sounds differ as pleasing or harsh.
Refined and common speech come together in the dark,
　　clear and murky phrases are distinguished in the light.
The four elements return to their natures
　　just as a child turns to its mother;
Fire heats, wind moves,
　　water wets, earth is solid.
Eye and sights, ear and sounds,
　　nose and smells, tongue and tastes;
Thus with each and every thing,
　　depending on these roots, the leaves spread forth.
Trunk and branches share the essence;
　　revered and common, each has its speech.
In the light there is darkness,
　　but don't take it as darkness;
In the dark there is light,
　　but don't see it as light.
Light and dark oppose one another
　　like the front and back foot in walking.
Each of the myriad things has its merit,
　　expressed according to function and place.
Phenomena exist; box and lid fit.
　　principle responds; arrow points meet.
Hearing the words, understand the meaning;
　　don't set up standards of your own.
If you don't understand the Way right before you,
　　how will you know the path as you walk?
Progress is not a matter of far or near,
　　but if you are confused, mountains and rivers block your way.
I respectfully urge you who study the mystery,
　　do not pass your days and nights in vain.

RESOURCES LIST

Nothing Holy About It: The Zen of Being Just Who You Are, Tim Burkett

Zen in the Age of Anxiety: Wisdom for Navigating Our Modern Lives, Tim Burkett

Returning to Silence, Dainin Katagiri Roshi

You Have to Say Something, Dainin Katagiri Roshi

Each Moment is the Universe, Dainin Katagiri Roshi

The Light That Shines Through Infinity, Dainin Katagiri Roshi

Zen Mind, Beginner's Mind, Shunryu Suzuki Roshi

Not Always So, Shunryu Suzuki Roshi

Branching Streams Flow in the Darkness, Shunryu Suzuki Roshi

Cultivating the Empty Field, Hongzhi (trans. Taigen Leighton)

Inside the Grass Hut: Living Shitou's Classic Zen Poem, Ben Connelly

Inside Vasunadhu's Yogacara: A Practitioner's Guide, Ben Connelly

Mindfulness and Intimacy, Ben Connelly

ACKNOWLEDGMENTS

Lyndall Johnson and Charisse Lyons. All my love and gratitude.

Tim Zentetsu Burkett. Nine full bows.

Dainin Katagiri Roshi and Shunryu Suzuki Roshi, two founders and teachers of American Soto Zen. I aspire to your Dharma example.

The past and present priests and sangha of MZMC, especially my friend of many years Ben Connelly, as well as Tomoe Katagiri, Ted O'Toole, Guy Gibbon, Lee Lewis, Bonnie Versboncoeur, Rosemary Taylor, Wanda Isle, and Susan Nelson. And my friend Kimberly Johnson, who holds it all together in more ways than anyone knows. All of you teach me the Dharma. *Gasshō*.

All the directors, mentees, companions, and fellow students that I've been blessed to walk the path with over the years. We all share the pilgrim's staff and teacher's fan.

The past and present providers of Aslan Institute.

My friend and spiritual brother Rev. Ward Bauman, and all at the Episcopal House of Prayer in Collegeville, Minnesota. You exemplify devotion, service, and the Spirit that knows no cage.

My friend, spiritual companion, and one-person support network and promotion team, Diane Millis. There would be no book without you, D, and I am so thankful for your example of lived faith.

My editor, writing mentor, and moral supporter, Rachel Shields Ebersole. Patient, wise, kind … and funny. Everything a new author needs. I tried to follow her wise advice, "Write the book you want to write."

Paul Cohen, Susan Piperato, Colin Rolfe, and all the good people at Monkfish Publishing. Professional, clear, respectful, and kind. I am indebted to you all.

Feedback readers, devoted Zen students, and general encouragers Amy Shinkō and Emily Strasser. Palms together.

Scott Edelstein, for his kindly and generously offered consultation, advice, guidance, experience, and laughs.

Norman Waddell for his translation of the Song of Zazen.

My parents, family, and friends. Thank you. I love you.

My sister Molly, whose fault everything is and always has been. Thank you. I love you.

My wife Karen, who is everything. Thank you. I love you.

And, finally, in no particular order: Grandma Hammond, the Soto Zen Buddhist Association, Stephanie Attia, Smith Coffee & Café, Mahapajapatti, Harriet Tubman, Barack and Michelle Obama, AURORA, Tillie Walden, Dessa, MST3K, Honda motorcycles, Sigrid, Archbishop Desmond Tutu, Highway 212 West, Pema Chödrön, *Unbreakable Kimmy Schmidt*, John O'Donohue, Thich Nhat Hanh, Fazerdaze, Rev. J. Phillip Newell, Cherokee Jack, Christos Center for Spiritual Formation, Mindy Gledhill, Barry's Classic Blend Tea, Temple of Heaven Gunpowder Tea, Rev. Zoketsu Norman Fischer, Rev. Shoken Winecoff Roshi and Ryumonji Zen Monastery, Willem Ibes, Joen Snyder and Michael O'Neal and Compassionate Ocean Zen Center, the Screaming Orphans, Paula Arai, Red Lyons, Phoebe Bridgers and boygenius, #FightForWynonna, my anonymous hospital bodhisattva, Eddie Izzard, Joseph Campbell, Rush, Howard Thurman, Doomtree, Duluth Harbor Cam, Made In Heights, Mississippi John Hurt, ARC Retreat Center, Hazel English, Maria Bamford, Lisa, Hobbes, the Vince Guaraldi Trio, 2218's Squad 41, Bomber Mountain, Hania Rani, Sally, Clara, Oliver, the authors of the First Amendment, the Teachers of America, and Bill W.

ABOUT THE AUTHOR

Busshō Lahn came to Soto Zen Buddhism in 1993, was ordained as a novice in 2009, and received Dharma Transmission in 2015. He is the guiding teacher of Flying Cloud Zen Spiritual Practice Community in Eagan, Minnesota, as well as a speaker, retreat leader, spiritual director, and senior priest at Minnesota Zen Meditation Center in Minneapolis. He also serves Aslan Institute, the Episcopal House of Prayer, and is as an Interfaith Fellow at Augsburg University in Minneapolis.

Busshō's teaching focuses on contemplative spirituality, twelve-step work, interfaith dialogue, mystical Christianity, and the marrying of spirituality with both Western and Buddhist psychology.

This is his first book. For more information, visit flyingcloudzen.org.